SUPERVISION IN COLLEGES AND UNIVERSITIES

Daniel James Rowley

Herbert Sherman

University Press of America,® Inc.
Lanham · Boulder · New York · Toronto · Oxford

Copyright © 2004 by
University Press of America,® Inc.
4501 Forbes Boulevard
Suite 200
Lanham, Maryland 20706
UPA Acquisitions Department (301) 459-3366

PO Box 317
Oxford
OX2 9RU, UK

All rights reserved
Printed in the United States of America
British Library Cataloging in Publication Information Available

Library of Congress Control Number: 2004111817
ISBN 0-7618-2988-1 (paperback : alk. ppr.)

∞™ The paper used in this publication meets the minimum
requirements of American National Standard for Information
Sciences—Permanence of Paper for Printed Library Materials,
ANSI Z39.48—1984

✼ Contents ✼

Preface		v
Chapter One	The Basic Concepts of Supervision	1
Chapter Two	Applied Supervision	21
Chapter Three	Strategies for Effective Supervision	41
Chapter Four	Strategies for Problem Solving	61
Additional Resources		85
Bibliography		87
The Authors		93
Index		95

Preface

In today's world, colleges and universities are facing major challenges. Society is moving out of the Industrial Age and into the Information Age on a very fast track. Technology is increasing at an explosive rate. International travel is commonplace as people throughout the globe become more and more comfortable with the emerging world economy. Resources are severely squeezed, and the demand for finding new and better ways of coping with this new world is everywhere. Many look toward colleges and universities for answers. These historic seats of wisdom have a tradition of researching and teaching that has always been a mainstay of societal understanding and development.

These facts have put a great amount of pressure on today's campuses, and not just in the laboratory and classroom. Everyone on campus is aware of the increasing demands they face as well as the squeeze on resources that every college and university experiences. This is why the topic of management in academia is so important today. There is growing interest in how campus managers (both academic and non-academic) do their planning, organize the resources with which they have to work, manage the institution's budget, and work with its human resources that either determines that a college or university will be successful or not. For all this, managers are held accountable, and success or failure rides on their actions.

As part of management, supervision is especially important because it is the management of individuals within a unit or department that often determines whether or not those individuals will be effective in their jobs, whether or not the department will contribute effectively to the mission of the campus, and to no small degree, whether or not the campus will fulfill its potential.

As we define it, supervision occurs in any situation where one person is responsible for the activities of others in a direct fashion. It is a department chair overseeing a departmental faculty. It is an accounting manager overseeing the work of a campus accounting staff. It is a head grounds keeper overseeing the activities of the grounds crew. It is also the campus president or chancellor overseeing the work of vice presidents or vice chancellors. The interchanges that occur between a supervisor and a subordinate, the skill of the supervisor to know how the duties of the unit or department should be carried out, and the ability of the supervisor to coordinate the activities of his/her unit or department with the rest of the campus all make a significant difference as campuses seek to survive in a growing competitive environment.

This book is intended to be a field manual for college and university supervisors. It looks at the activities of supervision in many areas of a campus, and provides an applied approach to help supervisors better understand what their responsibilities are and how to best carry them out. We begin by identifying the important theory base that comes from years of research into what methods of supervision work best, then adapt it to the special world of the collegiate supervisor. Beyond that, we look at specific topics of interest and concern and suggest a wide range of tactics that campus supervisors might use to be as successful in their responsibilities as possible.

There are four chapters in this book, along with a listing of additional resources following Chapter 4. In Chapter 1, Definitions and Concepts, we identify supervision as different from other types of work that occur on a campus. This chapter is designed for the novice who needs a solid grounding in the work he/she is now responsible for. In Chapter 2, Applications in Higher Education, we begin to apply the basics to the particular situations faced on college and university campuses. The mix of academic, administrative, and support functions all present different challenges, but must work together for the greater good of the entire campus. In Chapter 3, Strategies for Effective Supervision, we describe a wide variety of tactics that collegiate supervisors can employ to gain mastery over the challenges they face in their individual departments or units. And finally, in Chapter 4, Strategies for Problem Solving, we examine those areas on a campus and those situations that create problems for supervisors, their subordinates, and sometimes the entire campus. We also provide a variety of tactics for dealing with these problems when they arise.

If you are reading this preface, you are either interested in taking on a supervisory responsibility or you have already done so. We wrote this book for you as both an introduction and as a guide. We understand how important the responsibility of supervision is, and we hope this book helps current and future supervisors from all parts of the campus to better understand what they must do, and through that, help the campus realize its important mission.

Daniel James Rowley, Ph.D.
Greeley, Colorado

Herbert Sherman, Ph.D.
Southampton, New York

ಸಿ Chapter 1 ೧೩

The Basic Concepts of Supervision

Supervision in colleges and universities is the responsibility of developing and using human resources to provide quality education, support for students, service to the academic and local communities, and to support the creation of knowledge. More importantly, supervision is a special privilege. As a supervisor, a person is given charge of the most important resource an organization has, its human resource, and is asked to work with that resource to produce the organization's services or products. These are noble objectives.

With this special privilege comes a sacred trust. Supervision provides the opportunity to work with someone else's resource base and prove one's ability to improve it. In colleges and universities, this concept is not new. Certainly the privilege of teaching has always implied this sacred honor. But beyond teaching, working with others to help improve the institution and its human resource base is no less as noble or important and is a critical component of providing quality education.

Supervision is not like other organizational work. When most people are hired into most positions, they are hired because they have a particular skill they can bring to the job that helps the organization do its work. Yet, while campuses do hire many people as supervisors, it is also a very common practice to promote line individuals into lower level management positions. In essence, organizations reward someone for the work they have done by hiring them to do something else – namely, work with people who now do the work they used to do. This is typical in the American promotional system.

Unfortunately, one major mistake that most organizations make, is that there is an assumption that these newly promoted individuals can easily become supervisors. It's not the assumption that supervision is easy, but that rather, it is natural. However, this assumption comes with its problems. Just because a person has been good in one position does not guarantee that that person will be good in a position at the next level up – especially when one recognizes the skills and abilities needed to be successful as a supervisor. This is not to be confused with the Peter Principle where people are promoted to their highest level of incompetence (Peter & Hull, 1969). What we are emphasizing is that employee supervision requires a different skill set than non-supervisory jobs and that many new supervisors do not possess these skills.

We have assembled this book as a way of helping those who have supervisory responsibilities better understand what is required of them now as a supervisor, that was not required of them before, and what they can do to be successful. We hope to demonstrate that managerial work is different from other types of work, but it can be extremely rewarding for those who learn its nuances and rhythms.

The Activities That Make Up Supervision

The work of supervision involves the deployment of organizational resources to help the organization achieve its ends. People are a significant part of this important resource base. People are the instruments who actually do the work of the organization. Directing these resources and doing so in an effective way are the primary responsibilities of a supervisor. In this section, we outline the nature of this responsibility.

Supervision is a Form of Management (First Line Management)

The term "management" can be understood in many ways. For the purposes of this book, however, we believe that Certo's definition (2000) is most appropriate. He states "Management is the process of reaching organizational goals by working with and through people and other organizational resources" (p. 6). In this definition, there are a lot of different things going on that are meaningful. One, management is a process, a process that has no particular beginning or end. It is continuous. Two, it is the process of reaching organizational goals. Organizations survive because they accomplish their purposes for existing in the first place, and the easiest way of defining that purpose is through the setting of identifiable, measurable, and attainable goals. Three, management achieves these goals through working with and through people. In other words, managers (or supervisors) do not achieve organizational goals themselves, but work with and support those who do the actual work that reaches the pre-defined goals. Finally, four, management achieves these goals through working with and through other organizational resources.

Often, successful management is the result of not only skillful use of scarce resources, but creative use of those resources as well. Problem solving is a critical component of supervisory management and it is unlikely, however, that anything in a person's pre-supervisory position could adequately prepare that person for these types of responsibilities.

Supervision Concentrates on the Human Component

More specifically to supervision (as opposed to other managerial activities in an organization), supervisors work much more with human resources than with other resources. This is front-line management and it is extremely crucial to organizational success. Supervisors have more contact and influence with the working core of any organization than does any other type of manager. Here, understanding the nature of the resource, the capability of the resource, and then utilizing that resource as effectively (and perhaps as creatively) as possible is the primary responsibility of the supervisor.

The supervisor is also a part of the rest of an organization's management structure. First level supervisors are themselves supervised. Second level managers take on even more responsibility in that they not only have to supervise the people in their charge (exactly the same as the upper level managers do) but also they must integrate the activities of the department, or departments, that make up a larger responsibility area within the organization. This chain of command (a term coined by Taylor, 1947) continues all the way to the top of the organization – the Chief Executive Officer (a president or board chair of a business operation, or a president or chancellor in the typical academic setting). As one goes up the ladder, responsibilities go up, and as responsibilities go up, pay normally follows.

Yet, for the purposes of this particular book, it is also useful to remember that a campus president or chancellor, while fully responsible for the entire success or failure of his/her institution, is still a supervisor as well. This person most likely has a staff and a number of vice presidents or vice chancellors for whom she/he serves as supervisor. So it is important to understand that while management may take on different faces and responsibilities throughout any organization, there is always an element of supervision. Mastering this element is central, then, to effective management.

What is Supervision?

Getting back to the notion that supervisory management is a process, it is helpful to know what are the specific processes that characterize supervision. Below, in Table 1-1 we identify 5 general characteristics and 2 specific ones.

Table 1-1
Characteristics of Supervisory Management

- General Characteristics
    - Leadership
    - Managing human resource
    - Planning
    - Organizing
    - Evaluation and feedback
- Specific Characteristics
    - Part of a system
    - An on-going process

General Characteristics

We begin, then, by exploring those characteristics of supervision that are more universal and apply to all supervisors. These are some of the skills that were most likely not required of a person prior to selection as a supervisor.

Leadership. Leadership is an intensely personal issue – both for a leader and a follower. It is also crucial to understand (and all too many supervisors and managers do not understand) that any one given person cannot be a leader because she/he has decided to be a leader. Leadership is inextricably fused with followership (Barnard, 1938). In other words, followers choose their leaders; leaders do not choose their followers. This one central characteristic of leadership is so critical for managerial success that we will spend a great amount of time in this book describing the relationship that exists between a supervisor and an employee and why sometimes this is also a leader-follower situation, while other times it is not.

In this same vein, leadership cannot be commanded, it can only be awarded. Here is where many managers fail. If they command their subordinates to follow their lead, they will be disappointed at the results. Having the authority to supervise (the right to lead) does not necessarily create leadership (the ability to lead). The supervisor is compelled to earn followership in order to become a leader. This is the only way it works (Conger and Kanungo, 1998).

Assuming that a supervisor can become a leader[1], then the second part of the issue is what is the role of leadership. Most theorists in the field would agree that leadership is the ability to successfully direct others to accomplish some task or goal. Goldman (1998) has said that the major focus here is the human focus and the understanding that tasks are completed and goals are attained when leaders are successful in inspiring their followers to do the work, and to do it at the highest level of dedication and quality possible.

Still another central issue about the importance of leadership is that of helping followers cope with change. Scholtes (1998) has reminded us that as we move more definitively from the Industrial Age to the Information Age, that changes come more rapidly and are usually more severe in their effect. He goes on to point out that strong, capable leadership is absolutely required to help individuals and entire organizations recognize the need for change, help discover appropriate alternatives, and to lead through the change implementation process.

Human Resource Management. Much of the early study of management was done with the goal of improving structures and technologies to assure the highest returns to owners possible. Scientific Management (Taylor, 1947) was born in these early years, along with the framing of something called the Ideal Bureaucracy (Weber, 1947). The types of organizations that these early management theorists defined tended to be highly impersonal, rule-oriented, and dominated by top-down decision making. Other contributors to what is generally referred to as the classical school, were researchers such as Frank and Lillian Gilbreth who are credited with the development of time and motion studies; Henry L. Gantt who developed techniques such as Gantt charts to help improve efficiency on a scientific basis; and Henri Fayol who developed a list of 14 principles of management, including "unity-of-command" and "division of work" (Wren, 1994). Many of these ideas continue in the modern workplace, and many current managers are more comfortable with the formula-driven methods of management they offer as opposed to the behavioral ideas that emerged.

The Hawthorne Studies conducted by Rothlisberger and Dickson (1938) are generally credited with beginning a second major way of thinking about effective management. These researchers started the human relations movement that several other theorists have contributed to since. This is where

---

[1] There is a school of thought in the leadership literature that leadership cannot be taught and is a function of either personal traits or the fit between style of leadership and job characteristics. See Yukl, 1994 for a thorough discussion on differing theoretical perspectives on leadership.

much of the study of leadership, communication, motivation, and group dynamics became part of the ever-growing complexity of the management paradigm.

Today, our fundamental understanding of supervisory management is based upon all of the major research that has gone before. Many of the formula-driven approaches have been discarded, particularly when it was demonstrated that such approaches were generally dysfunctional in the face of complex and dynamic environments. But one of the areas where the field continues to put great store in is human resource management (HRM).

Essentially, HRM views the human resource as two things: people (sentient beings), and a resource (something that can be used to help generate desired outcomes). First, supervisors must understand employees are human beings, not machines. They are fallible, not perfect. They are capable of being involved, not emotionally separated from the firm they work for or the work they perform. They can be empowered, not programmed. Further, they are capable of followership and honest participation, as opposed to being self-serving and uninvolved. Most important, people are endowed with an abundance of creativity and a desire for self-expression through their work -- we are what we do and we value ourselves by how others value us and our work (McGregor, 1960).

For supervisors, this means that they must fully understand the capabilities of their human resources, and then act to optimize the use of those human resources. Simply, supervisors cannot do the job themselves *and* they should never try to. Instead, by understanding and working with the human resources within their charge, supervisors get into a win-win type of situation where employees grows (a win), the organization achieves its goals (a win), and supervisors reap the satisfaction of knowing that they have been a major reason as to why (a win) (Spencer, 1989).

Planning. Planning is one of the principles of management that continues to be a crucial topic, and planning is not normally one of those skills learned at operative levels of the organization. Planning is an integral part of departmental life and is best done in a participative environment, and although employees normally look toward their supervisors to learn what needs to be accomplished (goals as an example), they will need to be a part of the overall development of the direction the department will take over the ensuing period. Even so, it is still the responsibility of the supervisor to develop the planning structure that leads to the year-to-year and day-to-day activities that will define employee activities (Bittel, 1980).

Planning is a process. First, it involves knowing what goals the organization expects units to achieve. Second, it requires that the planner look at the best methods to achieve the goals: the options available; the costs involved; the human resources needed; the materials and support services required; the timing involved; and an understanding of what could go right as well as what could go wrong. This is data collection and analysis, essential skills supervisors need to master. Finally, once a plan is formulated, supervisors then must rely on their leadership abilities to implement the plan through their employees.

Organizing. The activity of planning begins the process of accomplishing organizational goals. The process of organizing helps effectively implement plans by creating structures in which to accomplish said goals such as reporting relationships (chain-of-command) and work processes (employee work flow) (Galbraith, 1977). Organizing is also the skill of understanding the processes outlined in the plan, understanding the capabilities of the resource base (both human and other), and then meshing them together so that the plan works. Taking an idea and explaining its design as well as the technologies that are required to accomplish it are the heart of organizing. These are uniquely crucial supervisory skills.

Evaluation and Feedback. When a goal is achieved, is the process over? When a job is finished, is it really finished? The answer to both, for a supervisor, is no. For unit accomplishments to be effective, a supervisor needs to be involved in two more activities, evaluation and feedback. Part of the supervisor's responsibility is to look at the events and analyze them to learn what went well and what didn't go as expected. It's important to remember that organizations are human in nature and that it is not possible to do things perfectly with people involved. The other side of this reality is that everyone within the organization has the opportunity to learn from what has happened, so that when they are faced with similar issues in the future, they can improve their performance. This is what is known as organizational learning.

Objectivity is the key to success here. It is perfectly natural to look at human fault as something that is either good or bad, and it is easy to assign emotional value to the results of events as we will examine further in Chapter 4. This is a very human thing to do. Further, these tendencies come through in the management process very easily. So, it is not surprising that many supervisors get emotional when things go wrong, or especially well. It's part of our humanness. Yet, one skill that supervisors need to develop and exploit is the ability to be objective and not emotional. In the next chapter of this book, we develop the techniques of transactional analysis, which describe how many of the behaviors of childhood development find their way into the ways we act with each other during adulthood. We will describe how difficult it is, many times, to be objective, as we advocate here. So, while we concede that objectivity is hard to achieve, we nonetheless contend that supervision (as well as management in general) is always more effective when objectivity is involved (Carroll and Schneier, 1982).

Regarding further the issue of effective evaluation and feedback, not only is it important that supervisors exercise as much objectivity as possible in looking at the results of performance, but it is just as important that they convey what they have learned with those who actually performed the activities. Objectivity and honesty are two of the keys that help build the trust that is necessary to create leadership. Objectivity and honesty recognize the pluses and minuses of the human resources base and provide a mechanism for improvement as well as a basis for distributing rewards. Objectivity allows the supervisor to view the planning and organizing processes as non-personal events and allows the course of learning to progress.

Specific Characteristics

While the above characteristics and activities are universal to all supervisors in all organizations, there are two additional characteristics of supervision that reflect the nature and character of individual colleges and campuses. These are the specific issues that make supervision different from one setting to another. These characteristics pose a different challenge for the supervisor. Here, supervisors have to understand the systems and environments of the organization they are a part of, and incorporate these into their overall skill set.

The Organization as a System. It's easy for people in organizations, regardless of their position, to become so wrapped-up in their own jobs that they forget what is going on in the rest of the organization. This happens as easily on college and university campuses as it does in business organizations, perhaps even more so given the structure of academic disciplines. Regardless, supervisors need to guard against parochial behavior and they must continually remind themselves that they have been given a responsibility to administrate only one portion of a much larger organization. Unless supervisors understand how their particular areas of responsibility feed into the whole, they will not be effective.

Further, they need to guard against any type of parochialism in their employees. This is where leadership becomes an important tool. Part of the message each and every organizational supervisor needs to share with subordinates is that what they do impacts the entire organization. This is called systems thinking -- it recognizes that each supervisory area is part of a whole that is dependant upon a common resource base, depends upon the same system of organizational communication, and whatever someone does is done in the name of the campus as a whole. These elements describe the internal environment of the organization or campus. Also, it is within this environment that the supervisor must fashion her/his methods of interactions with subordinates, superiors, and peers in order to be as effective as possible (Johnson, Kast and Rosenzweig, 1963). The unique circumstances of each organization and each unit setting will define the specific characteristics supervisors must develop to be effective in this area.

The Organizational Environment (Internal). Further, each organization creates its own unique internal environments that reflect the unique histories, beliefs, cultures, and traditions that mark each organization's methods of doing things. This impacts the work of supervisors just as much as the other characteristics we have identified already, because it means that each managerial situation is embedded in a system of operations that is comfortable, familiar, and predictable by most organizational workers. While this environment may not be ideal, and there may be good reason to challenge it or change it, this is a time-consuming process and there are limits to just how much change subordinates may be willing to endure.

College and universities are no different from other traditional organizations in terms of how influential and controlling their internal environments are (Gouldner, 1954). Academic cultures and structures create their own unique set of internal environmental forces. Figure 1-1 below, represents a general model of the organizational environment one might encounter on a typical college or university campus.

Already in the model are a variety of system factors we introduced in the last discussion. The complete model identifies the several additional components that contribute to the overall understanding of what factors contribute to the specific process of supervision. These include several important personal characteristic components. In a very real way, just as we identified as true for the organization, the responsibility of supervision is also a system. What Figure 1-1 demonstrates is that supervision is not simply an issue of skills, or even of the realities of the organization the supervisor is a part of, it is also an issue of what and who the person is who is the supervisor as well as who the supervisor is managing – its own unique system.

Figure 1-1
The Supervisory Process in Colleges and Universities

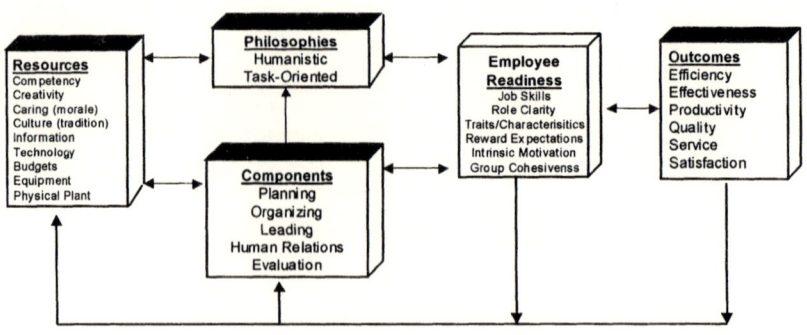

Feedback Loop

While we will spend a great amount of time in this book in discussing the importance of remembering that a supervisor's subordinates are human beings, it would be a clear mistake if we did not also recognize the humanness of the supervisor, which impacts much of how and why supervisors do what they do. Just as all other employees, the supervisor comes to the job with what the supervisor is; who the supervisor is; the knowledge base the supervisor possesses; the skill base the supervisor has accumulated; the belief systems that help create the supervisor's personality, ethical beliefs, and perceptions of others; creativity; tolerance; motivation; and temperament that will influence and help explain why he/she does what she/he does and why. This issue of humanness is crucial in understanding and properly managing the supervisory process, yet it is often down-played to the demands of the work itself. However, effective supervisory management not only recognizes this reality of organization, it uses it as a way to assure high levels of performance and goal achievement.

Further, the model in Figure 1-1 goes beyond the identification of the several areas where human behavior impacts the supervisory process and suggests a system of work, and several other components that help identify the internal environment of the organization. One of the other major issues is that of non-human resources. No organization has the ideal resource base it would design for itself. For colleges and universities, this is a particularly salient issue today as funding sources put more and more constraints on external revenue sources. All organizational managers must constantly adjust to the changing nature of resources, and in today's world must often respond to a reduction of resources (Pfeffer and Salancik, 1978).

In colleges and universities, the resource environment fluctuates and is highly unpredictable, and this has a major impact on the rewards with which supervisors can work with. In an ideal world, a supervisor would like to negotiate with subordinates for specific goal accomplishment and tie that to specific rewards. However, in the world of colleges and universities, it is often impossible to know what resources will be available, let alone knowing whether or not a supervisor might be able to commit them as much as a year in advance.

For example, in the State of Colorado, the State Legislature in the year 2000 mandated a new state employee evaluation and reward program called Peak Performer. State college and university classified employees are part of the State Personnel System, and therefore, were subject to the new law. The State put the plan in place early in the year, did extensive training for both employees and supervisors (in fact, it was mandatory training which had negative consequences for both employees and supervisors who did not attend), and by April 1st, all supervisors and their subordinates had spent an extensive amount of time goal setting, career planning, and filing those plans with the campus HRM offices. To be a Peak Performer, employees had to perform at specific levels, and upon receiving a Peak Performer designation, were to participate in a State-wide pool of merit money.

In July, the State announced that it had failed to find enough money to fund the merit pool. In late September, when both supervisors and subordinates were under mandate to go through a 6-month performance review, it was clear that the program would not be funded – period. One can just imagine the frustration involved for both supervisors and employees to go through the mechanics of a process that had no tangible reward attached to it, as originally promised. In 2001, when the first year was complete, the State Personnel System decreed that not only would the supervisor and subordinate need to go through a full year-end review, but would also need to prepare similar forms (already even more complex) for the next year, when it already seemed certain that there would again be no resources available to fulfill the program.

This example is one of many that represent the difficulties supervisors and their subordinates face when dealing with the uncertain resource bases that are common in colleges and universities. While not all issues are related to the evaluation system, this example is not too far from the difficulties that occur in the internal academic environment in issues such as budget cuts that reduce work forces; budget reallocations that take resources from one area and put them elsewhere on a campus; mandated use of resources with one vendor where other vendors might be able to supply campus needs at a lesser costs; running out of supplies; having to pay for hidden services (for example, the surprise technology charges that pay for a campus technology support system that departments may be unaware they were liable to pay for); and on and on.

Performance outcomes depend upon resources, the personal philosophies of supervisors and those in their charges, as well as the methods and activities of supervision. Further, as the model suggests, supervision is a process, not an event.

Finally, all elements in the model, are connected by feedback. This further supports the earlier discussion of the learning organization. It also demonstrates the importance for supervisors to constantly monitor and maintain control of an event to insure that both the supervisor and the subordinate learn from on-going activities to be able to insure that future activities will improve.

The Organizational Environment (External). The last area that defines the activities of supervisors come from the external environment. This is were one finds the key stakeholders of the organization. These are groups or individuals that derive a benefit from the activities of a college or university as well as those who provide needed resources to the campus. In Figure 1-2 below we have listed many of the typical stakeholders for a typical U.S. college or university (Rowley and Sherman, 2001; p. 215). These external people and groups often wield significant power that impact what supervisors do and how they do it.

Figure 1-2
Post-Secondary Institutions and Their Stakeholders
External Stakeholders

	Internal Stakeholders	
Competitors	Board of Trustees	Creditors
Government Agencies		Local Community
-accrediting bodies	Students (learners)	General Public
-funding agencies		Suppliers
Alumni	Faculty	-High Schools
Students (customers)	Administrators	Unions
-Parents		Professional Assoc.
Employers	Other Personnel	Philanthropists

Supervisors are most directly impacted by the college's internal management structure with whom they have day-to-day interactions and who have larger responsibility for the organization's resources. In terms of external stakeholders, supervisors may deal with certain external stakeholders on a daily basis (for example, cash flow is critical for a campus so that the Bursar's office may be in constant contact with lending agencies). In other cases, contact might be of a more temporary nature (as an example, department chairs working with accrediting agencies). There may be still other external stakeholders that are critical to their operation because of the strong dependency relationship the campus may have upon them (such as major contributors) (Pfeffer, 1982). Yet all of these can impact the responsibilities of supervisors and managers throughout the campus.

Who is the Supervisor and Who is Being Supervised in the Academic Setting?

Supervision becomes even more complex in colleges and universities when one begins to examine the several different types of supervisory relationships that exist. In the following discussion, we identify five specific types of relationships that exist and briefly describe the nature of each of these supervisory environments.

Academic Department Chairs Supervising Faculty and Department Staff. Perhaps one of the most difficult supervisory environments to describe, and one that is only found in the academic setting is that of the academic chair. Unlike most other situations, this one is tenuous, because the academic chair may either be a fully constituted supervisor (appointed with specific supervisory responsibilities and activities for a significant period of time) or a rotating chair (a faculty member elected as a department chair for a short amount of time, not too dissimilar from most campus academic committee responsibilities). For the fully appointed position, there is not much difference between the responsibilities of the chair and most other supervisors in both the academic and non-academic structures of the campus. This person will make personnel decisions, evaluation decisions, oversee the department's academic scheduling, assign coverage for classes, deal with student concerns, manage the support staff of the department, and a myriad of other responsibilities (depending on the nature of the individual departments).

The rotating chair is in a much more uncertain position. This person remains a peer of the other faculty members in the department, which significantly challenges her/his ability to deal with all of the same issues that would confront the more permanent chair we describe above. Faculty members thrive in an environment of collegiality and group decision-making. Yet, many of the activities of the chair challenge collegiality and require top-down choices. For example, when a chair is charged with evaluating faculty member performance and then is required to rank individuals based on that evaluation, collegiality is challenged. Further, ambiguity is introduced to the equation, given the reality that the current chair will be returning to the general faculty as an equal, and be succeeded by a faculty member who must now make decisions related to the former chair's academic performance. All of these make this type of supervisory situation uniquely difficult.

Academic Unit Heads Supervising Large Academic or Administrative Units. Deans, Provosts, and Vice Presidents or Vice Chancellors who are appointed to supervise large academic or administrative units create a second highly distinguishable supervisory environment. Further, since campus presidents or chancellors are generally considered the head of the academic and the administrative structures of the campus, they also fit into this particular environment. Normally, all of these folks are former faculty members, and it is usual for these individuals to have attained a Ph.D.. Yet, most of these people, though they retain their faculty status in many cases, are not considered faculty members by the rest of the faculty. They administer the institutional budget, make decisions about the configuration of the campus, and may also decide which members of the faculty will be retained or released. Often these activities create friction with the academic faculties, given the reality of tenure and the tradition of joint governance with the faculty.

To some degree, their decision-making is usually moderated, since there is the possibility that these supervisory individuals may return to the general faculty. On the other hand, these folks tend to exhibit a more traditional business management orientation than one might see with the department chair. They still have a tie to the academic side of the house that differentiates them from the non-academic supervisors one finds elsewhere on campus.

Administrative Department Heads supervising Department Staff. Beyond the academic side of the campus, there is a large management structure that oversees the administrative, campus service, and student service activities of the campus. Supervision in this portion of the campus tends to resemble the more traditional business-style activities and responsibilities that are common outside the academy. It is interesting to note that on many campuses today, many of these responsibilities have been out-sourced to traditional businesses to operate on behalf of the campus. All to suggest that the more traditional business norms and business ethics are common in these areas of campus life, so it is not surprising that more traditional supervisory practices are common here as well.

Research Department Heads supervising Faculty, Research and Department Staff. A hybrid of the supervisory environments we describe above, many major colleges and universities also support research centers.

These programs may take on any number of organizational forms, yet normally operate as independent profit-centers. Professional administrators manage them and perform similarly to administrative department heads supervising department staff. These centers adopt a unique business environment by hiring their own staff and research faculty and employing a project management structure. Each research project normally has a principal investigator (PI), with strong academic credentials, who reports to the supervisor of the research center. The PI is responsible for both the technical side of the project, the oversight of research team, as well as budgetary considerations.

The department head (as supervisor) is ultimately responsible for the center's ability to economically sustain itself and handles the business functions including employee payroll, grant administration, and interfacing with grant-funding agencies. A variation of this operation is to utilize faculty members from within the institution (from academic departments) as both research staff (through offloading of instruction) and/or as administrators (similar to academic department chairs). Supervision of employees in these research centers is strongly tied to the organizational configuration of the center and its relative use of in-house staff versus subcontracted or borrowed faculty/staff from other units from within the college or university. Research centers may, therefore, operate similarly to any of the prior configurations discussed or as a mixed operation. Supervisors of research centers must still pay particular attention to the human resource mix and its operation.

The Special Case – Supervising Students. Students represent an especially interesting challenge to the activities of academic supervision. First, students are temporary; second, they are only with a college or university for a time frame of approximately four years; third, they are usually only available during the normal 9-month school year; working is the secondary reason they are on a campus and may be less serious about working than other professionals on staff; and fourth, they are preoccupied with their academic activities and social activities. Students are learners first and employees second. Further, students come in a variety of academic commitment levels – undergraduate, masters level, and doctoral level.

Perhaps most important, students are also consumers of the college and university and must be treated differently than traditional employees. The principles of supervision continue to apply, but the application is extremely complex. When a supervisor fires or reprimands a student worker, the campus may lose more than merely an employee. Supervision here could be an issue for any member of the faculty, faculty administrators, support staff, and research heads.

We will develop all of these relationships throughout this book, and provide ideas about how to work in each supervisory environment to achieve the most effective results. At this point, it is important to understand that a modern college or university campus contains a wide variety of differing supervisory environments. This presents a unique set of challenges, but also presents a wide variety of opportunities to experience and optimize the supervisory experience.

How Does Supervision Work? (The Underlying Philosophies)

Finally, we look at the philosophical issues that characterize an effective supervisor. These are ideas that have been generated in both the Classical and Behavioral Schools of management theory, but have endured as fundamental principles about how the modern campus supervisor should view the responsibilities he/she has been given. Table 1-2, lists several of the philosophical predispositions that produce effective supervisors.

Supervisory philosophies may be broken down into two major elements: humanistic and task-orientation. (McGregor, 1960) *Humanistic philosophies of supervision* are based upon the fundamental belief that work is desirable, enjoyable, and an expression of human creativity -- the supervisor's job is to unleash the potential of his or her employees.

Table 1-2
Effective Philosophies of Supervision

<u>Humanistic</u>
Flexibility
Trust
Empowering
Developmental
Rewarding
Team Building

<u>Task-Oriented</u>
Oversight/Monitoring
Staffing
Organizing
Corrective Interventions

Flexibility: a supervisor needs to be flexible, both in terms of the work of the unit and in terms of the activities of subordinates. As we've described earlier, it's important for a supervisor to understand that subordinates are people, and each employee deserves to be treated as an individual (Peters and Waterman, 1982).

Trust: a supervisor needs to become an effective leader. As we suggested earlier, leadership implies followership, and followership occurs when followers trust the direction of the person they have chosen as leader. Beyond this, the supervisor needs to be able to treat each employee as a professional, someone who is capable of doing a job at a high level of dedication and quality. Trust works in both directions (Zand, 1981).

Empowering: each supervisor needs to learn the lesson that she/he cannot do the work by him/herself. Each supervisor needs to understand that the unit requires a variety of skills and contributions and that subordinates will work most effectively when subordinates learns to manage their own work. Empowerment means giving subordinates control of certain resources – their own decision-making power, and control of organizational resources to be as effective as possible in their responsibility area they work (Waterman, 1987).

Developmental: because supervisors recognize the HRM component of the unit they oversee, they also recognize that part of their responsibility is to improve their subordinates. Finding ways of improving employee skills, knowledge, and abilities; and allowing subordinates to take more of an initiative in doing their own work will help improve the human resource and benefit both the organization and the subordinate (Wexley and Latham, 1981).

Rewarding: employees must be recognized and rewarded for what they do. Certainly, as we indicated earlier, the supervisor may not be in control of the monetary resource base to be able to control monetary rewards, but the supervisor does have a responsibility for trying to assure that the employee will receive fair monetary rewards (certainly in proportion to the other constituents on campus). Further, psychological rewards are just as important as monetary rewards. Respect, praise, inclusion, and recognition are day-to-day rewards that cost nothing, but mean everything. It is surprising that so many supervisors, inside and outside the academy, find engaging in this type of reward system so difficult (Pinder, 1984).

Team Building: one of the most exciting aspects of managing is the ability to create something meaningful. Building a group of subordinates into an effective team is one example of this possibility. Simply, teams are more effective than work groups. Teams work together. Teams work for a common purpose. Teams seek to achieve higher goals, and teams build on motivation and make it even more important and effective (Fujishin, 2001).

Task-oriented philosophies of supervision reflect the need for the supervisor to both meet organizational goals (effectiveness, efficiency) and to develop a productive work unit. The supervisor's job is to ensure that his or her employees are obtaining both their individual and team objectives and to provide them the needed resources in order to help them accomplish their tasks (Odiorne, 1961).

Oversight/Monitoring: supervisors must approach the control responsibility cautiously. The notion of control can quickly escalate to out-of-control behaviors where all of the other philosophies, behaviors, and skills that have contributed to building trust are destroyed by punitive control behaviors. The proper philosophy to embrace is that of oversight and monitoring – the visual and intellectual understanding of what is happening, without the overt actions of confrontation in the face of performance that does not meet expectations. Oversight should lead to quiet evaluation, non-emotional and non-public analysis sessions between the supervisor and the subordinate where the supervisor and subordinate objectively evaluate performance and determine a solution that both feel will succeed.

Staffing responsibilities: once in place, a supervisor is responsible for the on-going staffing of the unit. People come and go – people act out their humanness. But the issue of staffing goes beyond hiring and firing (or overseeing transfers and retirements). Certainly, a supervisor needs to take the lead in identifying changes that will occur in the work unit, and be in a position to describe the skills and abilities the unit needs in replacements. This is also an issue of improving the current staff – recommending training, education, and other activities that will help current staff become more knowledgeable and effective.

Organizing: organizing is part of the basic function of supervision. Organizing requires that supervisors seek the most efficient and effective manner of using the unit's several resource bases. This is an integrative responsibility that requires that the supervisor develop a deep understanding of the capabilities of her/his resource bases, what the needs of the organization are for that unit, and then how the resources available can best meet organizational needs. This is also a whole new way of thinking for most new supervisors.

Corrective interventions: supervisors work with human subordinates, work under the authority of human managers that oversee them, and work within human organizations. Mistakes, and sometimes disasters occur. As a result, part of any supervisor's responsibilities is to recognize problems, analyze them as objectively as possible, and then take corrective actions. If the problem exists in the unit, in either a single subordinate or a group of subordinates, it may be necessary to correct their behaviors and activities. The supervisor has a variety of choices that range from the traditional parental punitive models to the much easier laissez-faire approaches. As we will suggest in Chapter 4 (and as we have strongly implied in this chapter), an objective approach is always preferable. Depersonalizing the problem allows everyone the opportunity to find the roots of problems and deal with them directly (Taylor, 1947).

In this chapter, we have introduced the many dimensions of supervision. In the next chapter, we move to a variety of discussions about the tools that are available to help the supervisor be effective on the job. We also develop the ideas of transactional analysis. As a philosophy, transactional analysis presents a very appealing approach to introducing objectivity and trust into the supervisory environment. That, along with the basics of supervision we have described in this chapter, the collegiate supervisor should be able to begin to develop a personal strategy for being the most effective supervisor possible.

ಞ Chapter Two ଛ

Applied Supervision

How should supervisors view and treat the people in their charge? This is perhaps one of the most important questions that every supervisor needs to determine when seeking to be effective in his or her position. In this chapter, we look at these concerns for academic supervisors. We begin by looking at a model of human interaction, called Transactional Analysis (TA). TA is an especially helpful tool for a supervisor's tool bag in that it provides an explanation of the roles we assume in our interpersonal communications and relationships, and identifies the types of relationships that work and those that do not.

Following this, we describe several of the relationships that exist in colleges and universities between supervisors and their subordinates in a variety of settings. By mastering these concepts, the academic supervisor should be in a powerful position to execute the needs of the organization through the human resource base for which she/he has responsibility.

Transactional Analysis

The field of transactional analysis has been around for about 50 years. Its aim is to show how people interact based on the roles and perceptions they have regarding themselves and others. Among others, Harris (1999) saw the usefulness of this model in the workplace, particularly because of the strong relationship between the actions of parenting and the actions of management. Family relationships are not too dissimilar from organizational relationships, and TA has proven to be a good method of viewing both of them. Figure 2-1 shows the basic transactional analysis roles.

Figure 2-1
The Roles in the Basic Transactional Analysis Model

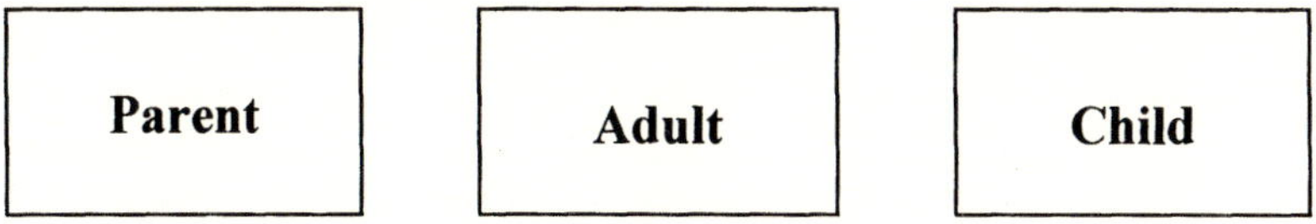

| **Parent** | **Adult** | **Child** |

The parent-child-adult model (PCA) is an excellent way of viewing personal interactions. It views the roles people assume in communicating with each other, and as the model demonstrates, it suggests that some of the transactions that occur when people assume one of the roles are more functional than others. There are three main roles here, the role of the parent, the role of the adult, and the role of the child. The model also suggests certain relationships and their effectiveness.

Role of the Parent.

The parent is a strong role in TA. It comes from the role all of us have experienced as children growing up. Our parents (or those who raised us) employed a system of formal and informal controls that allowed them to direct our actions, thinking patterns, cognitive development, and attitudes. These were care-giving people who nurtured us, protected us, corrected us, and sometimes punished us. The parent can show emotion, both anger, as well as joy and pride. Paternalism is a term often used to describe a good parent.

In the workplace, the parental role is alive and well. Since management is responsible for the organization, controls resources, and is responsible for the activities of subordinates, it is understandable that they might rely on their own parental experience as a model for how to get things done. Paternalism is accepted and sometimes even expected. Without other training (and as we explained in the first chapter, many managers and supervisors do not receive formal training for their jobs), we cannot be surprised that this model of supervisory behavior is pervasive.

The parental role is very common in colleges and universities, where the strong tradition of teaching (implying that the professor knows and the students learn from the professor). Secondly, the inherent hierarchical structure of a college or university lends itself to supervisors assuming the parental role (Brown, 1983).

Role of the Child

The child is also a very powerful role. Everyone has been a child and knows what children do. As a child, everyone has had the experience of not knowing what to do, depending on others, being nurtured, learning, being corrected, and being punished. Another one of the most important things that children do is play. As people mature into adulthood, these lessons learned and these tendencies, or predispositions, to act in certain ways continues as a strong influence.

In the workplace, it is easy to allude to the role of the child as the one many subordinates are in – either by choice or by circumstance. Often, the traditions of the organization speak to first-line employees as children – management makes all the plans, management makes all the decisions, management controls all the resources, and management has all the power. In this type of a setting (very similar once again to that which we find in colleges and universities), employees survive when they accept the child role and initiate little initiative or confrontational behaviors. The other circumstance is the choice to be a child – refusing to take the initiative, needing to be led, afraid of responsibility, often very emotional, and just doing the job.

This is not to suggest that the role of the child in an organization is bad. As we just described it, there are more negatives than positives (particularly in a setting where we want to support the full and effective use of the human resource), but the child also has that element of innocence and playfulness that can make the workplace less restrictive and an enjoyable environment to be a part of. The occasional office party, the sociable lunch hours, recognition ceremonies, and receiving rewards are all more meaningful when we let the child loose a little and enjoy the moment, laugh a little, and maybe even get just a little bit crazy. This is not only true of first-line workers, but supervisors and managers as well, all the way up to the campus president or chancellor.

The Role of the Adult

The role of the adult is extremely important in organizations, but the weakest of the three described in TA. The most striking qualities of the behaviors of the adult are that they are objective, honest, and fair. The adult tries to recognize what is true and to act accordingly. On the downside, the adult tries to act without allowing emotions influence decisions or actions.

In the workplace, interestingly enough, all the theory the field has developed and all the internal guides (such as rules and regulations, job descriptions, and job specifications) support an adult approach by every member of the organizational community. Yet, because every member of that same community is a human being, it is hard to avoid emotions, difficulties that lead to irrational responses, and desires to protect oneself (or make certain that one gets proper rewards). These emotions challenge the ability of every supervisor and manager to be completely objective all the time. Nonetheless, the reality is that the best supervisors are the ones who can be objective, honest, and fair, and therefore, this is a role that every supervisor needs to understand and try to emulate in order to be optimally effective in the position.

Inter-role Activities

The roles in and of themselves are interesting to note. However, one needs to view these from a superior-subordinate, interactive perspective, or role set. That is, both supervisors and their subordinates enact these roles simultaneously and thereby create a paired set of roles. Some of these paired sets are very functional (these are relationships that can work), some are very dysfunctional (people in these relationships experience a great amount of friction between them), while some can be either functional or dysfunctional depending upon the circumstances. These role sets are represented in Figure 2-2 below.

Figure 2-2
The Transactional Analysis Relationships Model

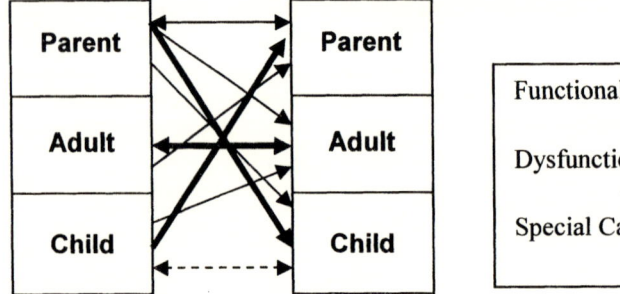 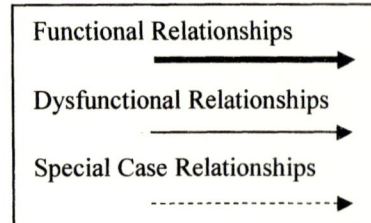

Functional Relationships

As the model suggests, there are three functional relationships or role sets: 1) one person behaving as a child in the presence of someone who behaves as a parent; 2) one person behaving as a parent in a relationship where the other person behaves as a child; and 3) one person behaves as an adult in a relationship where the other person also behaves as an adult. The parent-child behaviors are understandable and come directly from the parental-child experiences of growing up. Though familiar, and while they are functional, these relationships are not optimal for the organization and are considered unhealthy to the organization in the long run. For example, the child does not engage in innovation, creativity, or perhaps even honesty, so the organization does not get the full benefits of their skills and competencies. Also, the parent has to spend so much time directing and leading, that other activities go undone or are done less well.

The adult-adult relationship is different. Not only is it functional, it promotes the full use of the human resources in both the subordinate and the supervisor. The relationship is objective, honest, open, and innovative. These are major positives for both the people in the relationship as well as the organization. Everyone wins (a "win-win" relationship).

Dysfunctional Relationships

The model shows a variety of circumstances where the mix of the relationship results in dysfunctional operations and outcomes. When both participants behave as parents, there is obvious friction because neither party recognizes the authority of the other. When one participant behaves as a parent and the other as an adult, there is friction because both participants need a different type of response in their relationship that they are not getting. Here, because of the strength of the parent role, the normal situation is that the adult becomes the child in order to achieve some level of harmony (though resentment could be present). Similarly, when one participant behaves as an adult and the other as a child, friction again comes as a result of neither participant receiving the responses they prefer in their relationships. Often, the extreme power of the child is usually effective in forcing the adult into a parental position.

In colleges and universities, this tends to explain why it is hard to get students to take more of a responsibility for their own education. It is clearly easier for the student to allow the professor to teach predefined materials rather than to go out and seek additional opportunities for learning. Unfortunately, the same situation can also found in supervisory relationships throughout the campus.

A Special Situational Relationship: Child-Child

The model identifies one final relationship that can be either functional or dysfunctional, based on the circumstances. The child-child relationship is functional, when it is alright to play, and such circumstances exist. Time away from the office, parties, clearly social occasions, and being able to see the humor in a difficult situation are all made more enjoyable when the participants can be more child-like in their behaviors.

Child-child relationships can be disastrous when important work needs to be done. When no one in the relationship takes responsibility, uses imitative, or exercises dishonesty, results are never good. Whether it is in business or on a campus, supervisors need to guard against this situation completely because everyone loses.

Supervising to Achieve the Most Effective Relationships

It is the responsibility of every supervisor to make certain that the relationships that exist between them and their subordinates are as functional and as effective as possible. As we have described transactional analysis, it should be straightforward that an adult-adult relationship is the preferred method of achieving these ends. Yet, as we have also described, achieving an adult-adult relationship is hard because the other two roles are so powerful.

To achieve maximum effectiveness, a supervisor has to understand the dynamics of relationship dynamics, the power of the roles of the parent and the child, and then institute an adult-adult approach. Because of either their own personalities, or perhaps because of the campus's traditions of more parent-child relationships than adult-adult relationships, subordinates may not respond as hoped immediately. Patience, trust building, and the reward system are all allies of the supervisor in making positive changes. Finally, it is important to guard against the sudden slips – a bad situation that evokes a lot of emotion, especially anger. It is extremely difficult to be objective in the face of emotion, and this is clearly one skill that will help distinguish better supervisors from the rest.

How Does Supervision Work in Administrative/Academic Units?

Interestingly enough, supervision in an academic or administrative unit is not dramatically different from supervision in a professional service firm (i.e. legal, accounting, engineering, and medical, etc.). Each work unit is comprised of staff personnel (clerical and technical support) as well as in-house experts (faculty or technical experts) who provide educational or administrative services to the student learners. A typical academic unit is denoted in Figure 2-3 while an administrative unit is pictured in Figure 2-4.

Figure 2-3
Typical Academic Department Structure

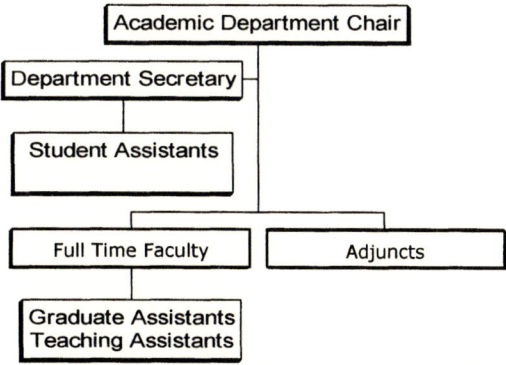

Figure 2-4
Typical Administrative Department Structure

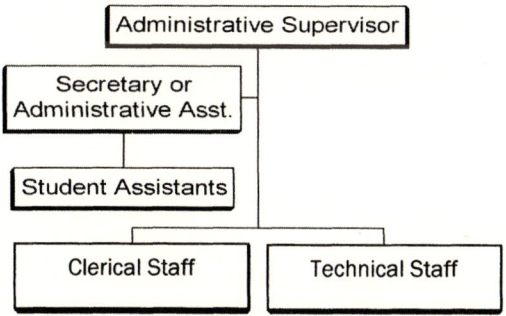

Supervisors are responsible for the day-to-day operations of their unit as well as for the productivity of the workforce they supervise. Firstly, supervisors are responsible for *planning* for their unit. At this organizational level, planning normally entails the translation of department goals and objectives into operating rules, procedures and policies; facilitating what Simon (1960) would call routine decision-making. For an academic unit, this may entail such tasks as course and faculty scheduling, arranging for book orders, hiring adjuncts, and student registration. For an administrative unit, this could involve student billing, processing financial aide requests, and obtaining proper IRS 1040 forms. Planning also involves working with each unit member to infuse departmental goals with personal goals, that is, making sure that members of the work unit are motivated to meet department objectives because it serves their own needs as well.

Second, the supervisor must *organize* his or her unit in terms of how work will flow through the department. Many times an employee will be designated as the "link-pin" or contact person with other units or the customer (in this case, the student), and that liaison person will then funnel the work to the proper person (or work team) – a hub and spoke system of work allocation. Other times, work is sequentially handled, that is, each person in the unit performs a specialized function within a work chain (or work process – sometimes referred to as value chain; Porter, 1985) and than passes the job onto the next employee until the work is completed. In other work settings, the unit members act as a single unit completing a task as a team or act completely independently of one another. From a faculty member's perspective, much of their instruction-related work is highly autonomous in nature. Regardless of the task structure, the supervisor must coordinate its operation and ensure proper workflow.

Supervisors must understand what *motivates* their unit members and then manipulate the existing compensation systems and the job design, in order to maximize employee effort and performance. In administrative units, the ability to create autonomy, flexibility, and challenge is crucial for enhancing job performance. In academic settings, where compensation may be fixed (such as one finds in union contracts and/or administration policies) and perhaps of less interest to some employees, supervisors may have to tap into higher level motivators (belongingness, self-esteem, achievement/self-actualization) in order to allow employees to create more challenging and interesting jobs. Certainly faculty would prefer higher salaries, however, they may also react favorably to off-loaded instructional time for research and course development, favorable course scheduling, and travel funds.

Supervisors must set a good example for their employees – role model the behaviors (and indirectly the values) that they think are critical to the success of their operating units. Supervisors *lead* their employees not through charismatic speeches but by work performance and facilitating the work of others. Employees respect supervisors who do as they say and not ask employees to perform tasks that they themselves would not do. Without belaboring the point, administrative personnel have little respect for those supervisors that talk team spirit but practice authoritarian rule.

This is especially true for faculty who expect to be treated with deference and handled with the utmost respect. They are experts and wish to be treated appropriately -- they will not be lectured to in terms of office collegiality. Their expectations are that everyone will conduct himself or herself in a professional manner.

Last, supervisors must make sure that the work processes and procedures actually result in the proper completion of assigned tasks – that the objectives for the unit are being met (if not exceeded). This *monitoring* or control function also involves changing workflow on a continuous basis (called continuous improvement), and may require the supervisor to rearrange their operating unit (i.e. new operating procedures, employee retraining, job enlargement, job enrichment, and self-managed work teams). Faculty members are especially sensitive to peer and student instructional evaluations as forms of performance assessment devices.

Professors and Instructors Are Not Naturally Supervisors

Many administrative supervisors have argued that since faculty members must manage their classroom (even in an internet or distance learning setting) and their research projects, that faculty members perform numerous supervisory functions. Even without the United States Supreme Court ruling that disavowed faculty as management, faculty do not act in a supervisory capacity (unless acting as an academic and/or research unit supervisory) in their functions as instructors, researchers, committee members, and student advisors. Professors and instructors provide educational services to the student learner and the more general academic community and therefore are equivalent to line workers – they have direct contact with students and provide after-sales service to them (Porter, 1985). Therefore, faculty members are equivalent to the technical staff in an administrative unit that provides student services.

The real irony is that many members of the faculty neither want to be supervisors nor want to be supervised. Many instructors see the role of administration as buffering (Thompson, 1967) them from the annoyances of running a college or university. At its best, administration facilitates the teaching and research processes by providing the resources, facilities, and technologies necessary to achieve academic excellence. At its worst, college administrations become the bane of faculties' existence by foiling their every attempt to accomplish their lofty goals and objectives. Most academics would prefer to have nothing to do with college administration since administrators clearly do not understand faculties' motives, needs, and expertise.

Many academics dread the day that they must assume the department chair's position (many colleges and universities rotate the position so as to share this responsibility). His or her colleagues may in fact consider an academic turned administrator either a turncoat or an incompetent. Many wonder aloud, why would someone want to enter the ranks of administration and give up their teaching and research?[1] What possible motive (except power or greed) could be attributed to a colleague who forgoes the robes in place of a suit and/or a desk job? Again, many academics hold administration in rather low regard and would tend to shun those academics that sought administration positions.

Supervision is a **Staffing** Issue

If supervision in academic units do not directly involve faculty then who does the unit manager supervise on a daily basis? Every academic unit has staff assigned to them (secretary, administrative assistants, student workers) and the daily work of the academic unit is accomplished through staff personnel. The job of staff members in an academic unit is to minimize the faculty's burdens in running the department. To say that staffers are a critical component of the academic unit would be an understatement – the staff does everything from answering the department phone (which some faculty detest doing), routing students to their correct faculty advisor, ensuring that faculty have the proper resources and equipment in order to teach their classes, processing payroll and other expenses, photocopying, etc. Without the proper operation of this support staff, the unit could become a disaster.

Supervision in an administrative unit is much clearer cut in that the unit in question has a designated set of responsibilities and functions. Again, the clerical staff provides support for the technical staff of the unit by handling the more routine requests and freeing up the technicians to handle exceptions to the rules (Galbraith, 1977).

How Should Administrators (Non-Academic Units) Supervise Non-Academics?

There are no real differences for supervising non-academic units than managing in a business or not-for-profit environment. Technical personnel of the unit (for instance, admissions counselors in an enrollment services office) will be fairly well educated, highly motivated, and consider themselves self-starters. They normally require only general guidance and expect to be given great independence in terms of carrying out their tasks. Administrators are

---

[1] There's an old adage – those who can't do teach; those who can't teach administer teachers.

cautioned not to over supervise these personnel in that they flourish when they can problem solve on their own.

Clerical staffers are usually also fairly well educated and their talents are more in knowing how to deal with the college's bureaucracy than the particular subject of their technical counterparts. They have developed their own communication network, sort of an informal communication channel that assists them in supporting their administrative unit. For example, although admissions counselors may be expert as to how to market their college (inquiry management, promotional strategies), their clerical counterparts will know exactly what administrative forms need to be processed in order to print brochures, place advertisements, and input inquiry information. Clerical staff members also tend to stay longer at a particular job and therefore have a longer organizational memory than their technical complements. Again, the clerical staff tend to require minimal supervision in that they are dealing with a bureaucratic system that they have developed a great deal of expertise about.

Trusting the Staff Person

Given our experience as both administrative and academic supervisors, we have come to understand what many experts have been saying for years - that trusting your technical and clerical staff is the most fundamental principle of supervisory management in an academic environment. We define to trust as the ability to allow others to perform their tasks and functions without direct interference from the supervisor – to let people do their jobs in they own fashion (within the limits of the procedures and rules) with the belief that if left alone to do their own thing that they will successfully complete their work. Trust also includes developing an organizational climate where workers will take initiative (risk) and act creatively in order to solve on-the-job problems. This requires allowing employees to make mistakes and to learn from those mistakes, what Peter and Waterman (1982) called championship behavior.

We understand, however, that the premise behind our need for trusting employees is that the employees are ready and capable of acting as professionals. However, this may not be the case for some employees. Whether due to stress, burn out, laziness, lack of trust caused by previous supervisors, or downright negativity, there will be some employees who will not work well in an environment where they are left to their own devices to complete their work. This is an unfortunate reality of any work setting, including academics. These individuals will reduce the effectiveness of the unit and act as barriers to change. From the supervisor's point of view, these individuals may seem self-centered, incapable of working as an integral member of the team, a constant wrench in the works, and a major source of every day frustration. Supervisors might even feel that these people live to make the supervisors' lives more challenging (or miserable). So how can a supervisor manage the unmanageable?

Working Around the Staff Person

Because many academic environments are unionized, it may be difficult to do the obvious with a resistant worker (Hersey and Blanchard, 1993) – fire them. Many supervisors try to transfer them to other units, units that may have less direct contact with students or may perform less vital functions for the college or university. If transfer is not possible, many supervisors may limit the scope of these individuals' jobs, in essence, shrink their jobs to a point where they can do the least amount of harm possible to the unit. One author has also seen the exact opposite happen, where the employee was so encumbered with additional work that the supervisor hoped that the employee would transfer or quit the job entirely.

However, all of these methods seem to overlook the need to confront the worker and find out exactly why they seem resistant (or performing below accepted norms). In many cases, poor worker performance is a function of lack of understanding his or her role on the job, low reward expectations, lack of job training, and fear of change (Steers, Porter and Bigley, 1996). In these situations, the supervisor can work with the employee to overcome barriers to work performance and therein increase employee productivity and job satisfaction.

Creating Trust in the Staff Person

Trust is not given, it is earned. This is certainly the case for a new unit supervisor where the employees on-the-job have already proven their capabilities and the supervisor has not. Our experience is that supervisors will earn the trust of their employees by demonstrating two things:
1. *Job competency*: supervisors not only know their own job but also know all of their employees' jobs (Taylor, 1947).
2. *Employee empowerment*: supervisors act as facilitators by providing workers with the authority and the tools in which to complete their tasks. In essence, the supervisor must first trust the employee to do his or her job before the employee will trust the supervisor to do theirs (Barnard, 1938).

We acknowledge that trusting first is a very difficult concept and may in fact seem quite Pollyannic. To put your managerial faith in a group of subordinates may in fact seem sacrilegious and fly in the face of logic and common sense. Further, for some supervisors, it is very hard to let go of control because they believe that they are the only ones who can properly do the job. Yet effective supervision is the ability to magnify the work performance of others (not to substitute your labor for that of your employees') and that only through trust can worker performance be maximized.

The Importance of Feedback

Feedback plays a vital function in supervisory management – it allows the supervisor the opportunity to reinforce both positive and negative behaviors of his or her employees while simultaneously reducing the workers' task uncertainty and ambiguity. Constant feedback and dialogue strengthens the trust between the supervisor and the employee by allowing the employee to seek greater understanding of the task at hand, expressing sentiment concerning the job, and reducing employee fears concerning job stability and continuity.

Avoiding the Parent-Child Situation

It is easy in traditional hierarchical settings for supervisors (and especially with their clerical employees) to fall into the parent-child transaction. The need to dictate and control is inherent in any chain of command and supervisors in an academic setting will need to guard against these tendencies. Furthermore, the less motivated clerical employees may certainly adapt a child mode of behavior in an attempt to elicit a parental response from the supervisor. Whether the employee is conscious or not of their enunciated role, the supervisor must maintain an adult approach and not seek equilibrium by changing to the parent role.

Maximizing the Adult-Adult View

Competency, trust and the job autonomy are key factors for ensuring that supervisors and employees will transact in an adult-adult manner. A supervisor can reinforce adult-adult behavior in his or her transactions by remembering to actively listen to his or her employees and to act as an advisor and/or sounding board for the employee. The supervisor must avoid the "telling" trap – that is, imposing his or her views on the employee in such a manner that the employee feels compelled to adopt them. Adult transactions require that disagreements be handled in a confrontational manner where both parties are perceived as having equal power or say on both the methodology for resolving the outcome as well as the outcome itself.

The Importance of Goal-Oriented Behavior

When supervisors and employees have disagreements, often it surrounds the methodology of completing a task or job. The authors subscribe to the concept of equifinality, that is, that there are many ways in which to solve a problem or to arrive at the same conclusion or result. That being said, the authors feel that supervisors should concentrate their efforts on assisting their employees achieve their designated goals rather than focus upon which methodologies are used to achieve those goals (Latham and Locke, 1979).

Why focus on goals? Numerous studies have demonstrated that those employees who have clear and concise goals and who are given the resources to achieve those goals inevitably outperform those employees who focus on processes, policies and procedures. Researchers have noted that employees who have and set goals feel greater ownership of their jobs and more work satisfaction.

Finally, employee accountability is far more effective when quantifiable goals are employed to evaluate employee performance. The focus of the assessment then deals less with "does the measurement instrument really measure my performance" and more on "whether I made my goals or not and what can be done in the future to help me achieve those goals." If compensation can be tied into goal achievement (this may be more difficult in a union environment), then productive employee behavior can be reinforced.

How Should Academic Administrators Supervise?

Being an academic in a supervisory position presents its own particular challenges. In one way, this type of responsibility is antithetical to the reasons most people worked to achieve doctoral status. Most wanted to be researchers, writers, or educators. Only a small handful would have achieved a doctorate to become administrators on a college or university campus. Yet, because of the crucial need for good management in the academy, and because of the desire of academics to be supervised by other academics, many faculty members make their way into the managerial ranks as departmental chairs, deanships, academic vice presidencies (or vice chancelleries), provost appointments, as well as presidencies (or chancelleries). In every one of these positions, there are supervisory responsibilities.

The basics are still there. Academic supervisors should attempt to engender adult-adult relationships. They need to be concerned about the motivation of the people who report to them, and seek to maximize the human resources for which they are responsible to maximize organizational outcomes. Yet because the principles of collegiality are ingrained in the structure of academic activity, academic supervisors also have to make supervisory decisions that do not damage either the academic environment of the campus (or portion thereof) and their ability to maintain collegiality as an on-going member of the faculty. This means that the academic supervisor faces more significant challenges than his/her counterpart in administrative supervision.

Is There Any Special Privileges or Knowledge that Comes With a Ph.D.? In the issue of supervision, very simply stated, no. The gaining of a doctoral degree denotes several accomplishments, all of which the recipient should be duly proud of. The new doctor is recognized as an expert by the larger academic community, and is given the privilege of helping to educate others, engages in the search for knowledge, and acts as an expert in counseling and consulting with others. Clearly, however, this expertise does not transfer over to the supervisory function although several Ph.D.'s may deem otherwise. Unless they attended a rather innovative Ph.D. program (or had prior managerial experiences), there are no special privileges or managerial proficiency earned via a doctoral education in terms of supervisory skills.

What this means for department chairs working with fellow faculty members, departmental staff, student assistants, and others beyond the department is that they must view themselves as novices (unless they have prior work experience) when working with their human resource base. Further, they must recognize that the best methods of getting the best contribution and performance out of that resource base is to do so from a position of collegiality – each relationship is an equal relationship (regardless of whom they are with), where contributions are valued, honest, open, adult-adult, and part of a growth process.

Team-Building and Effective Supervision. We believe that one of the major positive outcomes of academic supervision is the opportunity to be creative, to use the opportunity to supervise others to build a better academic environment. Team-building is one of these positive outcomes (Dyer, 1977).

From the opportunity to act as a departmental chair, to serve as a dean, or as a major campus academic officer, each supervisory position has the opportunity to either build a brand new team (when openings occur) or to use campus resources to improve the current work group. While capital resources may be scarce, the human resource, particularly in an academic environment is rich and opportunity-laden. Through participation, those within an academic supervisor's care have the potential of using their expertise, motivation, and innovative capabilities to accomplish department (school, college, or division) long-term goals. As we have suggested earlier, viewing the HRM base as a resource and using participatory activities to work with that resource are win-win situations for everyone involved.

Trust-Building and Effective Supervision. Both authors have had first-hand experience in terms of dealing with the issue of trust surrounding academic management, having been on the staff of a university president and having served as academic department chairs. They have learned that it is not unusual to have a fair amount of distrust inherent in academic supervisory situations. It was the experience of both authors that the exercise of position power and control of resources (plus a long history of problems between central administration and the general faculty) tended to reduce collegiality between different levels of campus administration and tended to spur on the politicizing of decision-making. This led to a feeling by academic administrators that certain faculty members were devious, self-serving, and counterproductive. These were hardly trust-building situations or environments.

Yet in these situations, as in the general environments that are typical on a large number of campuses, objectivity suggests other forces at play. Two explanations seem particularly salient. One is that of tradition, and the traditional imagery of a campus president. In the 1960's film, *High Time* (the story of a non-traditional student who goes to college to achieve a degree, long after he, Bing Crosby, had raised a family and grown a very successful restaurant business), the college president presents us with a fairly stereotypical role. The president is male, older, lives on campus, has a delightful wife, makes hard decisions, takes the hard line, is cautiously kind, and is absolutely in control. This paternalistic view of campus leadership is both appealing (knowledgeable, authoritarian, yet kind) and disturbing (dominated by rigor, duty, and tradition). In today's world, this type of president isn't particularly popular – yet it is surprising how many college or university presidents and chancellors try to fit that traditional mold *or* are placed in that role by on-going faculty and staff. The longing for *High Times* may infuse many academic environments yet today.

Two, many academic administrators feel that their positions and responsibilities force them into roles that they associate as more business-like than academic. They then tend to behave as they believe successful business supervisors and managers behave. As we described in the PAC model at the beginning of this chapter, the belief that successful business managers act in a profit-oriented manner, concerned for the bottom line above all else, and someone who believes that people are simply workers, can lead to a pattern of behaviors that emulate those beliefs. These resulting behaviors have nothing to do with collegiality and furthermore are not indicative of the business models employed by the successful organizations in the 21st century. Today's most successful firms espouse transformational leadership which includes employee empowerment, the creation of self-managed work teams, fostering creativity, investing in human resources (training), and crafting a learning, competency-driven organization (Peters, 1997).

Academic administrators' references to business models that are purely top-down driven (parent-child), what McGregor (1960) would refer to as Theory X style of management, are rather archaic in nature and should not be the ruling principles in devising academic supervision or management. Supervisory responsibilities do not imply stereotypical business approaches nor do they guarantee mutual dedication and objective resolution. This is why it is important that academic supervisors at all levels strive to achieve collegiality and adult-adult interactive relationships in order to help assure that optimal outcomes occur for everyone involved in the decision-making situation. This also happens when there is mutual respect and trust.

When supervisors make mistakes, they need to be open about it and to not try to find a scapegoat to pin failure on. In other words, academic supervisors build trust by being open, forthright and owning their decisions. Given the two major forces for acting in other ways that we described above, engaging in trust-building is certainly difficult. Yet, the benefits of team-building and trust-building provide many more opportunities for achieving high level goals than do lesser behaviors.

HRM and Effective Supervision. There is nothing more true than the reality that everyone in a college or university professional core is a human being. Each one has both positive and negative characteristics, but each possesses skills, talents, and abilities that can significantly add to the success of the many campus activities, programs, and central goals. Academic supervisors have the opportunity to find the unique talents of those in their charge and to then plan, organize, and implement those resources to achieve the highest level of positive outcomes possible in his/her area of responsibility.

However, there is another side to this issue. It is important to recognize the role of power in any organization, let alone that of colleges and universities. Power talks. People with power tend to set the model that everyone else sees as the trend to follow. If upper levels of management do not espouse the HRM approach to management, it is very difficult for lower level managers and supervisors to go against the grain. While we believe that acting in an honest, trust-building, team building, adult-adult manner is always superior to other forms of managerial behaviors, without the support of upper-level managers, the academic supervisor might feel somewhat isolated. Clearly, this is why upper-levels of campus-wide management need to buy into the principles we present here, because power talks.

How Should Academics Supervise Other Academics?

Given the above discussion, it would seem fairly obvious that the Golden Rule (treat others as you yourself would wish to be treated) applies when managing in an academic setting. All of the employees below the first line supervisor are experts in their own fields and deserve the respect of the supervisor because they have earned it through the most traditional of academic methods – completion of a dissertation and continued research in their own fields.

Non-supervisory academics, on the other hand, must also recognize that many of the administrators in an academic institution are themselves academics. There is a fine line between who is an academic and who is an administrator in that many administrators (college presidents, chancellors, academic vice-presidents, deans, department chairs, etc.) have quite an academic reputation. Collegiality must extend in both directions for management in an academic institution to be viable; faculty must accept the competency of their administrators as fellow academics while administrators (especially first line supervisors) must accept the expertise of their faculty. Without collegiality and common courtesy, administration within an academic setting will be calamitous.

Peer Supervision Has its Own Set of Pitfalls

Before we leave this topic and this chapter, we must point out that peer supervision has its own inherent difficulties. The prophet will not be recognized by his own people and familiarity breeds contempt – both of these sayings cut to the quick concerning the problems associated with chairing an academic department. It is very difficult for academics to follow anyone, no less a colleague from their own department. Faculty members who know each other's work and have worked with each other on a regular basis tend not to appreciate their associates.

Secondly, it is very difficult to supervise coworkers who one day may have the pleasure of being your supervisor. This may inevitably lead to politicking and possible inequitable treatment of junior faculty. Many faculty members discredit departmental peer review assessment instruments because they feel that fellow department faculty cannot remain objective.

Regardless of the particular department's circumstance, the department needs to develop a culture that nurtures participative management. That is, regardless of who is the chair for the moment, that decisions be made in as democratic a process as possible. This will provide for an open forum and allow all parties a say in the decisions of the department. By continuing a tradition of egalitarian academic decision-making, the negative attributes of peer supervision can be minimized.

Honesty and Integrity are Always Sacred Cows

Management, unconcerned of context, must deal honestly and virtuously with its employees. Adam Smith (1776) believed that only when men of good intention entered freely into a contract could an economic system that benefits both parties arise. We too believe that the underpinning of any working relationship in an academic setting is one of saying what you mean, and meaning what you say.

There is no management theory or management system that espouses dishonesty as a long-term supervisory method (even Machiavelli said that one must at least appear to be a good king). We have witnessed at several institutions how duplicity and lack of trust have hindered a college or university's ability to cope with the competitive market of the 21st century – plans cannot be developed in an environment where information is withheld for personal gain.

Although the prisoner's dilemma denotes human nature as self-serving, it is only the trusting prisoners who realize that if they work together (by not selling each other out) that they will both go free. We in our academic communities must also worked together, supervisors with faculty and employees, in order to form a partnership that will better serve our students and ensure the survival of our academic institution.

⁂ Chapter 3 ⁂

Strategies for Effective Supervision

In the last two chapters, we introduced the basics of supervision in an academic environment; the components of supervision (leadership, HRM, planning, organizing, and evaluation); the differing types of employees to be supervised (faculty, technical and clerical staff, researchers, and students) by two differing types of supervisors (administrator, faculty, researcher); the underlying philosophy (including flexibility, trust, empowering, developmental, rewarding, and team building); with specific applications to the higher education. We also introduced transactional analysis as a method that helps supervisors understand interactions between themselves and their employees through role enactment (parent, child, and adult) and how supervisors should react in order to create effective transactions (adult-adult). We then discussed the similarities and differences between academic and administrative supervisors and the implications of their managing either fellow academics and/or a technical and clerical staff.

Now that the foundation has been laid for supervision in an academic environment, we turn to the specific skills and strategies that supervisors might employ in order to effectively manage their academic or administrative unit. The remainder of this book then will focus on those competencies necessary to bridge the theory of academic supervision discussed in chapters one and two with on-the-job practice.

What Skills are Needed to be an Effective Supervisor?

In general, the types of skills supervisors need are represented in Figure 3-1 below as suggested by Katz (1974).

Figure 3-1
Categories of Skill Sets for Employee Supervision

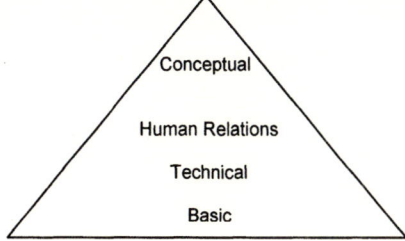

```
            /\
           /  \
          /Conceptual\
         /            \
        / Human Relations\
       /                  \
      /     Technical       \
     /                        \
    /        Basic             \
   /_____\
```

Basic Skills

Basic skills are those that historically have been called the "3 R's" (reading, writing, and arithmetic). These are the underlying skills that form the ability to complete a task at its most fundamental level. For today's supervisor, we might add to those skills computer literacy, which in the 21st century would include word processing, spreadsheet, database management, e-mail communications, and surfing the internet. Without these basic skills, it is difficult to not only supervise others (and be able to understand the skills they need) but to perform non-supervisory tasks affiliated with any job in an academic environment. Here, the expectation is that supervisors will already possess these skills prior to their assuming a supervisory position and/or will obtain these skills quickly as part of their job training.

Technical Skills

Technical skills are the specific job-related skills associated with the supervisor's position. For example, a department chair is expected to perform such tasks as course and faculty scheduling, recruitment and hiring of full and part-time instructors, budgeting, and student advising. An assistant registrar, on the other hand, might be required to evaluate transfer transcripts, audit senior transcripts for graduation, update computer codes for new majors and degree programs, and update the college catalogue (on-line or in batch mode) to reflect program changes.

Since technical skills are job-specific, we do not discuss the differing skills required per type of job except to note that all jobs require some engagement of technology and resources to manipulate and transform information in order to solve problems. A supervisor's position, however, must also include the technical skills of his or her employees. The supervisor must be able to perform his or her employees' jobs utilizing the same equipment and resources of his or her subordinates in order to achieve similar results (Taylor, 1947). This is not to suggest that the supervisor will actually do the work that subordinates are responsible for – rather having these skills oneself allows the supervisor to assist if needed as well as to provide standards which she/he understands.

Human Relations Skills

Thompson (1967) describes the supervisor's job as buffering the technical core (the employees) from outside disturbances either from within the work group, the organization as a whole, or from the external environment. It is human relations skills that set supervisors apart from their employees since it is the supervisor's responsibility to create a harmonious and productive work environment through his or her interactions with the employees. Specific expertise related to human relations skills include:
- listening and good communications skills
- truthfulness and honesty
- inspiring trust
- being human and appreciating humanness in others
- objectivity.

Listening and good communications skills. Supervisors must demonstrate their ability to listen to their employees. Listening starts with the development of an environment where employees feel comfortable initiating communication with the supervisor. Supervisors need to create a warm and friendly ambience where their employees know that their opinions are both desired and have value. Whether it is through a formal open door policy or through informal behavior, employees must feel that the supervisor is approachable and is willing and able to work with his or her employees to help solve their problems (Howell, 1982).

So how does an employee learn that a supervisor is accessible or not? Very simply, through the actions (or inactions) of the supervisor. First, supervisors who hide in their office and/or have minimal contact with their employees may believe that they have a very effective group of labourers. However, they may not have any idea as to what is actually transpiring in their office (Blake and Mouton, 1980). In order to be good listeners supervisors might practice a little MBWA (management by walking around), remembering that, like children, their job is to be seen, not heard (Drucker, 1977).

It is important to give employees the clear opportunity to talk about job-specific issues. Supervisors need to show that they care about them and the work they do. Supervisors also need to instil confidence in them so that they will not be hesitant to begin a conversation if there is a problem or an issue that needs to be discussed. If all supervisors do is walk around issuing orders, they will likely create an environment where people may well try to duck their heads and disappear whenever the supervisor shows up.

If MBWA is not possible, supervisors might initiate other forms of communication (e-mail, telephone) with their employees and do so on a regular basis. Distance may make the heart grow fonder but continuous contact will provide employees an opportunity to more effectively impart information and demonstrate an open channel of communication (Mintzberg, 1975).

Second, once an employee has begun a conversation, how the supervisor reacts to comments or suggestions will either positively or negatively impact further communication. There is an old adage about the messenger bringing the king bad news. Most employees will hesitate to tell the supervisor bad news if the supervisor's past reactions have been negative. Therefore, the manner in which supervisors handle bad or distressing news will send a clear signal to their subordinates about their approachability.

Even in responding to mediocre or good news, the managerial response (both verbally and body language) will show whether the supervisor is really open for comments or not. Employees are usually quite good at picking up on whether their supervisors are actively processing what they are saying or whether they are merely paying them lip service. To be a good listener, a supervisor must intelligently participate in the conversation; let the employee lead the conversation while the supervisor demonstrates that he or she understands what the speaker is saying and that they are really thinking about the issues or problems being raising. Listening, really listening, is crucial to employee supervision.

Being truthful and honest. In higher education, as we have stated earlier, supervision tends to go beyond single departmental issues. College and university supervisors must remember that they as not only role models for their employees but also as role models for the students who attend their institutions. Although honesty is always the best policy, it is quite surprising how difficult it is for some supervisors, when trying to convey negative information, to be completely honest and truthful. Many supervisors have a difficult time being open and honest perhaps due to the fear associated with hurting someone's feelings and possible reprisal to their downbeat comments. This type of avoidance behavior, however, is counterproductive and does not allow the supervisor and the employee the opportunity to discuss problems and to reach mutually acceptable solutions (Timm and Peterson, 1986).

Supervisors are professionals in the academic environment and need to understand that the culture of academic institutions, especially those of its faculty. Most value honesty and truthfulness. Plagiarism and cheating are not tolerated by the faculty and college administration and similar behavior by first-line administrators is unacceptable (McKeachie, 1986). More importantly, honesty and truthfulness are elemental to any interpersonal relationship and form the basis of a trusting relationship (Carvell, 1980).

Inspiring trust. William Ouchi's (1981) Theory Z, documented trust as one of the central themes in Japanese style management. Ouchi contended that Japanese firms develop a powerful bond between workers and management by running the firm on a family basis - one based upon mutual trust. Effective managers are those who inspire loyalty, hard work, long hours, and high quality production in their workers. They treat their workers with dignity and respect. Time clocks are banned. Managers and workers are on first-name bases, and all eat lunch together in the company cafeteria. Further, top managers brief employees on sales and production goals and employees are encouraged to be completely open in their comments.

The Japanese style of management has forced U.S. business to become more competitive and strive for excellence (Peters and Waterman,1982). Many American business have done this by adopting a management approach that decentralizes decision-making, fosters entrepreneurial thinking, rewards team building and team problem solving, and in general values the worker above being merely a cog in the machine. In essence, U.S. firms have rediscovered a more realistic potential for their employees and that the best way they could unleash their employees' work potential was to trust employees to do their jobs to the best of their abilities.

So how does a supervisor inspire trust? Halloran and Benton (1987, p. 421) noted that trust could be developed by following this fairly simple do's and don'ts list:

Do: assume trust initially (until proven otherwise), communicate openly with others, share information (not evaluation), display confidence in others' abilities, earn trust, make and keep commitments, respect everyone, operate with honest and integrity.

Don't: take cheap shots, knowingly hurt another, talk out of both sides of your mouth, talk behind backs, use scapegoats, second guess others, doubt when listening, play games with peoples' jobs and careers, and take organizational matters personally.

At the simplest level, in order to inspire trust, supervisors must invest their trust in others. Investing trust goes way beyond the spoken and printed word and involves the actual behaviors of the supervisors. Trust is not created through declaration of trust through e-mails, phone calls or memos but by the day-to-day actions of supervisors as they work with their employees. Employees know if they are trusted and will return that trust in-kind.

Being human and appreciating humanness in others. One of the authors of this text is reminded of his father's reaction to his undergraduate academic performance. For his freshman and sophomore years, this author maintained a 3.5 grade point average (GPA). Without any feedback from his father, this author then obtained a 4.0 GPA for his junior and senior years. Finally, mentioning this mark of accomplishment with pride to his father, this author was asked, "and what happened to your first two years in college?"

The point to this little story is that people are human -- they have flaws, make mistakes, have bad days, learn at different rates, resist change, and sometimes can be downright annoying. Rather than pointing out their shortcomings, supervisors should be grateful for their efforts even when they are not always as successful as the supervisors want them to be. Understanding the humanness of others, (as well as ourselves) and cheering them on in spite of their foibles, is a important attribute of any supervisor.

Peters and Waterman (1982) call supporting employees "championship behavior" - that there are no failures, only learning experiences. We recommend this passage from Peters and Waterman's (1982) text *In Search of Excellence*:

> *Treat people as adults. Treat them as partners; treat them with dignity; treat them with respect. Treat them-not capital spending and automation-as the primary source of productivity gains. ...There are hardly a more pervasive theme in excellent companies than respect for the individual. (p. 238)*

This passage further reminds us that the same holds true for how supervisors treat themselves, that their expectations of their own performance should allow for their own mistakes and their own limitations.

This is especially true for supervisors who, according to David McClelland (1961), may have a high need for achievement. These types of individuals will only obtain satisfaction from achievement itself and will perform poorly in routine or unchallenging jobs (Steers, Porter, and Bigley, 1996). Supervisors need to create a work environment where being human means being humane to themselves and others.

Objectivity. Objectivity can be defined as the ability to step outside one's personal situation and biases, deal with the facts of a situation, and make fair and sound judgments. This is certainly one of the most difficult human relations skills to develop since it requires the capacity to be simultaneously empathetic, to see the big picture (discern a problem as part of a larger system), to balance the needs of differing individuals and the organization, and to make a fairly logical decision (Barnard, 1938).[1]

In terms of developing a systems view of a situation, we would certainly agree with Carl Weick (1979) that everyone has his or her own unique picture of the world (what he calls a causal map) and therefore, true objectivity

---

[1] Objectivity integrates human relations and conceptual skills and therefore is a more difficult supervisor aptitude.

is impossible to achieve since truth is in the eye of the beholder. However, we also agree with John Rawls (1971, p. 517) who argues that we should attempt to be objective for in that attempt we will frame our "conceptions and judgments from a shared point of view" and therefore reach mutual understanding and agreement. The point of view to which Rawls refers is derived by the supervisor from the stakeholders of the organization (see Figure 1-2, Chapter 1) - more specifically, the people (employees, students, faculty, staff, and others) that the supervisor interacts with on an everyday basis.

Clearly, caring about the customer (being concerned with others' needs), and recognizing that everyone the supervisors work with is their customer, is a major cornerstone of objectivity. One cannot be objective if one does not care about and/or know who he or she serves. Second, the ability to make an equitable decision is based upon respecting the values and the rights of those affected by the decision - the old adage of treating others as you yourself would like to be treated is apropos. Third, employing facts and using previously agreed upon decision-making tools will elevate decisions from opinions and guesswork to informed choices. If people can agree on the facts of a situation and the methodology for analyzing it then they can usually reach a reasonably rational decision (Gitlow, Oppenheim and Oppenheim, 1995).

Conceptual Skills

Conceptual skills are those proficiencies that allow supervisors to see their units as part of a larger system, to understand the linkages between that unit and other units, to understand the unit's relationship to its stakeholders, and to comprehend the internal operations and intricacies of his or her own unit (Kotter, 1978). Conceptual skills include the following attributes:
- planning: developing goals and objectives
- organizing
- creativity
- problem-solving/decision-making
- translating knowledge into action (implementation)

Planning: developing goals and objectives. Planning for supervisors is a process that translates the organization's goals and objectives into unit goals and objectives. These tactical plans implement the college's overall strategy for achieving their goals by creating unit policies, procedures and rules which embody the spirit of that strategy (Ellis and Pekar, Jr., 1980). Policies, procedures and rules create clear action programs or pathways for achieving unit objectives by reducing employees' task uncertainty (Galbraith, 1977). These plans define what's to be done and how it will be done.

For the purposes of our discussion here, the terms objectives and goals are interchangeable. Either term reflect the desired outcomes for individuals, groups and organizations and they provide direction for decision-making and criteria against which outcomes are measured. Clearly, colleges pursue many objectives simultaneously and from an operating unit's standpoint their goals must be aligned with the goals of the university (Odiorne, 1965).

Goals and objectives are not what the operating unit says it is going to do but what they actual try to accomplish. Real objectives are evident in the action that organization members engage in. For example, colleges and universities can claim that they are committed to providing state of the art quality education. However, if their information technology unit replaces its computers only when funds are available (rather than on a specific replacement cycle), then the stated goals are not the actual goals. Supervisors must be very careful to set goals that are realistic, obtainable, measurable and aligned with both the needs of the college and their employees. This will require working with their employees in order to create goals that are not only mutually agreeable, but also goals that will motivate the worker by stressing the importance of his or her job (Barnard, 1938).

Organizing. Organizing is the ability to create a formal framework by which job tasks are divided, grouped, and coordinated. A supervisor designs the work conducted in her/his unit by manipulating five key elements: work specialization, chain of command, span of control, centralization and decentralization, formalization, and work flow. The challenge is to design a work unit that facilitates effective and efficient work as employees strive to achieve organizational goals.

Work Specialization. Work specialization, or division of labor, is the degree to which tasks in an organization are divided into separate jobs. Work process requirements and employee skill level determine the degree of specialization. Supervisors try to match skill level with task requirements to maximize effectiveness. Work specialization further impacts performance by using repetition of tasks and appropriate training to improve employee productivity.

Chain of Command. The chain of command helps employees know to whom they are responsible, and whom to go to with a problem. There is an unbroken line of a authority that extends through the entire organization. Supervisors normally occupy the first position (or lowest position) within this chain that grants them authority to give orders and in return for the responsibility or obligation to perform to expected activities. Unity of command (only one boss for each employee) within the chain helps prevent conflicting demands being placed on employees by separate bosses.

Span of Control. The term span of control refers to how many employees a supervisor can effectively and efficiently handle. Usually supervisors tend to have larger spans of control (or management) than their superiors because decision-making at higher organizational levels becomes more unstructured and complex. Also, the more training and experience employees have, the less direct control over their activities is needed.

Centralization. Centralization is the degree to which decision-making is concentrated in senior management's hands while decentralization is the extent to which decision-making authority is shared with lower-level employees; more specifically supervisors.

The current trend in business is toward providing first-line supervisors broad latitude in decision-making. As competition intensifies, and the need for organizations to be responsive increases. This has made employees, especially who are closest to customers, extremely important. They are an excellent source of knowledge and implement changes that directly impact performance. Giving this group more input into certain decision-making activities can result in increased firm performance.

Formalization. Formalization influences the amount of discretion an employee has over his or her job. It is the degree to which task are standardized and employee behavior is governed by rules and regulations. In organization with high degrees of formalization, job descriptions, and standard operating procedures (SOP's) provide clear direction. Where formalization is low, employees have a great deal of freedom in deciding how they conduct their work. Within the same organization, different departments may have different degrees of formalization. In a college, professors may be told what subject to teach, but may have freedom in selecting books, materials and methods for instructing the course. However, the college maintenance staff has a strict schedule for cleaning buildings, mowing lawns and painting dormitories (Pfiffner and Sherwood, 1960).

Work Flow. Work flow, that is, how work is transferred from one employee to another, is a newer concept in organizing in that it examines the relative task interdependence of each employee. The typical production line approach, sequential interdependence, has the work flowing from one employee to another in a linear fashion with the employee at the end of the cue having the greatest dependence on the other workers. Pooled interdependence (also known as mutual dependence), on the other hand, uses a team approach where all of the employees must work together in order complete a task or function. Also, independence refers to a work flow where the employee can complete the work on his or her own (Mintzberg, 1979).

Creativity. One of the most overlooked conceptual skills, creativity taps into one of our most salient but unmeasured assets, our intelligence (Hage and Powers, 1992). We define creativity as the ability to imagine scenarios that have not occurred, to envision new ways in which relationships and patterns of social organization can be restructured (Hage and Powers, 1992).

Osborn (1953) believed that creativity was America's competitive edge earlier in the 20th Century. He felt that leaders should encourage creativity in that it: produced a wealth of ideas, improved interpersonal relations, motivated the workforce, and leveraged luck. More importantly, creativity is a fundamental component of problem-solving. The solution to many problems exists outside of the daily routines, rules, regulations and SOP's and requires out-of-the-box thinking. Creativity allows supervisors to deal with the ambiguity and uncertainty of the work environment by going beyond the here and now (the known) and imagining how the work might also be completed (Galbraith, 1977).

Problem-Solving/Decision-Making. What separates a supervisor from any other employee in an administrative office (or in an academic department), is that supervisors have the responsibility to solve problems by making decisions. The old adage that a problem isn't a problem until it is your problem, is not only true but cuts to the very heart of the matter. As a conceptual skill, the most interesting element in problem-solving is the recognition that one even has a problem (Elbing, 1970). In order to act on a problem, supervisors must be not only intellectually open, but also proactive

We describe problem-solving in greater detail in Chapter 4. However, based on some of the work by Halloran and Benton (1987, p. 204), here we provide a simple outline of the process of problem-solving (or decision-making) as follows:

1. Problem identification = defining the problem.
2. Problem investigation = researching the problem.
3. Solution design = devising the method in which a solution will be reached.
4. Data gathering = collecting information as per the solution design.
5. Data analysis = studying the data (sometimes employing statistical techniques) in order to discern trends or patterns which caused the problem.
6. Developing alternative solutions = creating possible answers to the defined problem.
7. Choosing a solution = weighing the pros and cons of each alternative to determine which one would best solve the problem.

The underlying assumption behind the above description is that supervisors try to make rational, logical decisions while considering all of the possible solutions. Simon (1976) noted that although we try to be rational, in many cases we *satisfice* (p. 38-41). That is, we make decisions that are not necessarily the best but are good enough to solve a problem. We take the path of least resistance (Lewin, 1951) because we do not have all the time, energy, resources or ability in which to develop the best answer.

Translating knowledge into action (Implementation). If decision-making describes how we solve problems, then implementation describes the actions we take to implement the solutions we have developed. Implementation is the deployment of organizational resources (staff, systems, structure, style, skills, shared values, and strategy) in order to enact decisions (Peters and Waterman, 1982). From a college supervisor's perspective, resources may include such items as budgets, information systems, union personnel, copying equipment, and a friendly style of managing.

Implementation goes beyond the deployment of resources. Supervisors must also be facilitators. They must create a work environment that enhances employee performance and nurtures self-development, as we discussed earlier regarding human relations skills. Creating this learning environment is important to facilitate implementation since implementation inevitably means change. Employees naturally resist change and the supervisors' role in overcoming that resistance is paramount to job performance.

How Much Time is Required to be Effective?

Efficiency is often the primary objective of managerial supervision (Taylor, 1947). Yet, it is interesting to note that many supervisors do not use their own time efficiently. There are often many parts of a supervisor's job that are unscheduled, as well as parts that are. Because of the need for a supervisor to be available to both subordinates and superiors, many supervisors find they have little control over their time. They compensate for this by working longer hours, by taking work home, or by trying to combine tasks. All of these actions can make the role of the supervisor much less rewarding, and often can also lead to high levels of anxiety or perhaps health problems.

The college or university campus is no haven from these tendencies, and in some cases, tends to amplify them. The pressures for quality and quantity, in an era of tight resources makes the supervisory job in an academic setting seem all the more difficult.

Supervision Is Time-Consuming, But Need Not Be All-Consuming

There may be some basic truths of good supervision that tend to escape the new supervisor. One, having been an operative-level employee and then having been promoted to a supervisory position, the person may not be comfortable with the idea of not doing operative work. Perhaps sitting at a desk all day and going over reports or planning for unit activities is so different from his or her previous experience that the new supervisor periodically goes back to continuing previous responsibilities. After all, those are responsibilities that are familiar, comfortable, and for which the person has already proven she/he can do successfully.

Two, there is a basic conflict between unscheduled time and scheduled time. Wanting to please both subordinates and superiors, often the new supervisor will not exercise control over his/her own time. Emergencies occur all the time – yet what is one person's emergency might not be a departmental emergency or require that the supervisor drop everything and run to be of assistance. For example, some students might think that they are having an emergency because they can't get into the classes they want. They expect the department chair (or perhaps the dean) to drop everything and assist. It is not uncommon, in many of these cases, for the chair or dean to drop whatever else he/she might be doing (regardless of its importance), and try to help – because the student is the customer! The reality is that these types of emergencies aren't emergencies at all. These are situations that can be dealt with in a timely manner, and might best be handled by setting an appointment at a time when both the student and the chair (or dean) can more logically address and solve the issue.

Three, as we have stated throughout, supervisory work is significantly different from other types of work done in an organization or on a campus. It runs at a different beat. It occurs at a higher level. It consists of greater responsibilities. Further, it requires much more creativity and patience than other work that occurs.

So, how does one view time, and how should supervisors structure the most effective use of their time? Two items suggest potentially good solutions. One, it is clearly important for the new supervisor to understand the nature of the job (Mintzberg, 1975). New supervisors must understand specifically what their responsibilities entail. From this will flow a better understanding of what is important and what is not so important, which allows individuals to move to the second item below.

Two, it is important that new supervisors learn to prioritize. Understanding that no one person can (or should) do everything, prioritization allows supervisors to get the most important things done first, lesser important things get done next, and finally, the least important things done last, providing they need to be done at all. Scheduling can be a major aid in helping to assure that priorities are carried out in a competent manner. Few operatives schedule their time (that is done for them by other, perhaps the very nature of the work). However, supervisors need to schedule their time, based on priorities, to assure their effectiveness.

Developing a Resource Mentality

The effectiveness of the supervision is inversely related to the time spent supervising. Another major key in being a good supervisor is learning to let people do their jobs. This is a resource mentality that, unfortunately, often gets overlooked as supervisors experience the pressure of getting the job done on time and at a high level of quality.

Once again, the Theory X view vs. Theory Y view comes into play (McGregor, 1960). In a Theory X world, managers assume that their workers are lazy and must be constantly monitored and pushed along. This is horrendously time consuming and seriously under-utilizes the expensive human resource. In other words, this costs money, which could be much better spent elsewhere.

On the other hand, in a Theory Y world, managers assume that workers are not only capable of doing a good job, but anxious to do so. All workers need here is a direction and adequate resources to produce services at a high level. The amount of time taken to provide direction and assure adequate resources is far less (particularly once the supervisor has established good skills as a planner), and the results of the work are of high quality.

The real problem here, of course, is that many models of management and supervision in academia are of the Theory X variety. For the new supervisor who wants to be effective, it takes a serious effort to move to a different orientation about the nature of people. It takes active participation in the selection process to hire only the brightest and the best. Also, it takes trust-building relationships to assure that the supervisor uses the human resource to its maximum advantage.

Selection Is Time-Consuming, But Crucial in Developing a Good HR Base

One of the major responsibilities of supervisory management is that of selection (Dunnette, 1966). Supervisory management must make decisions about the quality of the people the organization or campus hires. Once again, this is a tremendous opportunity for any campus to improve it human resource base, an opportunity not to be taken lightly. The primary objective of selection is to find and hire the most qualified available individuals who want to do the job. To be successful in accomplishing this goal, supervisors need to understand the theory of the position they are filling. By theory, we mean that supervisors needs to understand the tasks, duties, and responsibilities the job entails as well as the specific qualities, talents, and skills needed to do the job at the highest level possible. These are called job descriptions and job specifications, respectively. This does not mean that every new person a supervisor hires will be the optimal hire, but it does assure that the campus should be able to hire the best available person who, over time, can prove to become the most advantageous hire. It's also important to remember that the competition for highly qualified people is fierce, especially in several crucial areas of the academy.

Certainly, particular vacancies on college and university campuses cannot be filled by the supervisor alone (while others may be depending upon governance policies and rules). Searches, overseen by committees of faculty and/or staff are not uncommon for certain campus positions. However, the supervisor whose unit has the vacancy needs to be an integral part of the process (as the rules allow).

For example, there would never be a prohibition against the development and implementation of a well defined job description or specification, which a supervisor could help assure was used to guide the process. True, in some situations there may be laws or limitations as to the ability to change certain hiring and qualification guidelines – but the authors of this book are completely unaware of any such laws or guidelines that prohibit academic supervisors from searching for and hiring the best qualified candidate for a position.

Monitoring Should be Overt, Not Covert

As one of the major responsibilities of supervision, monitoring is the activity that helps supervisors know whether or not the work of the department is being done at a high or low level of quality. However, although monitoring has to occur, the issue is _how_ it should occur.

Once again, one of the major keys in monitoring is that both the supervisor and the subordinate fully understand the responsibilities and expectations of the job (Griffin, 1982). The primary person who will monitor performance is the employee, the person charged with completing the work. If the campus hires competent employees, then a high level of trust should exist. Subordinates will feel free to tell the supervisor when problems occur and can also routinely provide information on how things are going.

To further aid managers in developing effective monitoring techniques, supervisors can learn to watch for certain signals (called critical incidents) that demonstrate the need for intervention (Carroll and Schneier, 1982). For a department chair, having a series of students come to the office with the same concern about an instructor is probably a sign that there is a problem that requires personal intervention. Likewise, if a chair never hears anything about a particular instructor, this most likely means that there is nothing untoward going on. Backed up by a history of trust and other normal monitoring devices, such as a student survey, it becomes clear that leaving this instructor to do her/his teaching without interference is the best approach.

The key here is to assume that the person is doing the job, and doing it right, unless otherwise indicated. Yearly evaluations will confirm what the supervisor already knows or will allude to the need for greater monitoring.

Ah, but what about the problem employee? Shouldn't there be special monitoring put in place for him or her? Of course – but it is important to understand that problems generally show up all by themselves. A registration clerk who is constantly absent, comes in late as a rule, or who engages in inappropriate language or activities will quickly draw the supervisor's attention. At that point, the supervisor and employee can come up with a plan of corrective action and both go back to their primary responsibilities (Carroll and Schneier, 1982).

Take Time to be Honest and Appreciative

One of the best methods for building trust and loyalty is to be honest in one's relationships and by showing appreciation whenever appropriate. As we have stressed throughout, honesty is an imperative of effective supervision. An old saying suggest that sometimes the truth hurts. In reality, dishonesty hurts even more. Are we suggesting, then, that it is perfectly alright for a supervisor to be unkind? Not at all. What we are suggesting is that supervisors must be honest in all their relationships with both subordinates and supervisors.

We are also suggesting that there are many choices in how the supervisor demonstrates honesty. The supervisor can choose to be brutally honest – acting as a vindictive parent with an errant child. The supervisor can also choose to be apologetically honest – apologizing in a child-like manner for having to deliver bad news to a more domineering parent (and in the TA model, some supervisors do act this way in delivering bad news to employees, actually placing their employees in a parental role – a dysfunctional role relationship). Or, the supervisor can choose to be objectively honest – stating the facts and being careful not to allow feelings or emotions play into the delivery of the news.

As we've stated earlier, this third approach is the hardest approach. However, it is also the best. Over time, people begin to appreciate that objective information is the most likely to provide optimal solutions. In developing an atmosphere where honesty is respected and not feared, people feel freer to be more innovative and to challenge activities or events about which they are concerned.

In regards to showing appreciation, this is one of those tools of success that many supervisory managers overlook, and in some cases, actually resent. It's not the business model, or dare we say, it's not the macho model (Sargent, 1983). Some supervisors believe that having the job is reward in and of itself, and that having to reinforce expected behavior with praise or other intangible rewards is a waste of time and resources.

This is unfortunate and it is also altogether very common. Showing appreciation with a smile or a positive comment is highly motivational (Steers, Porter and Bigley, 1996). It tells employees that their work is recognized and appreciated. In almost every case, this will lead to even greater effort on the part of the subordinate to maintain standards or improve them. And what did this cost? How much time did it take? The expenditures here are negligible to nonexistent. And what were the benefits? Here is a classic case of win-win, where the employee feels value and where the campus sees improved standards and performance.

Does Supervising Others Take Away Too Much From the Rest of the Job?

We know that as one goes up the chain of command, the amount of time that the individual spends on supervising employees decreases given the need to focus on long-term goals and objectives. First-level supervisors should spend more time monitoring their employees than their higher level counterparts (Katz, 1974). However, well-trained and motivated employees require supervisory intervention only when there are exceptional circumstances to the work routine (Galbraith, 1977). The short-term perspective of supervision espouses closer supervision while the regular nature of the employees' tasks generate few task uncertainties.

It is the nature of supervision then to have supervisors not dealing with their employees on a regular basis in a substantive manner, unless exceptional situations arise. So, while direct supervision should be considered a major component of the job, it should certainly not be the only set of activities with which first-line supervisor are involved. This is also true for academic supervisors, such as faculty chairs, who spend a good portion of their time teaching, performing research, serving on committees, and participating in community service.

What is also normally true about administrative and academic supervisors is that the level of responsibility attached to their positions is greater than of those over whom they are responsible. For example, a secretary in the registrar's office may compile a computer-generated list of possible graduates while the registrar takes responsibility for ensuring that every graduate on that list has met the college's requirements for graduation.

Plan to Supervise at Appropriate Times and in Appropriate Places

Inevitably, to paraphrase a common expression, one should not necessarily supervise often but one should supervise well. The key to proper supervision is dealing with the issue of timeliness by developing an understanding of when employees may need and want supervisory assistance. Since all employees are different, and work in their own manner, there are not hard and fast rules in determining when a supervisor should take an active role in an employee's task performance.

Many effective supervisors subscribe to the notion that supervisors should be seen but not heard when it comes to their employees' daily tasks although they certainly may frequently offer words of encouragement. Stated another way, supervisors should be present in spirit and mind but not necessarily physically hovering around employees as they perform their daily functions. If an employee is having difficulty and providing that the supervisor has developed a developmental culture (an open door policy), the employee will feel comfortable approaching the supervisor when the employee knows she/he needs help (Bittel, 1980).

Another technique that helps create the proper working climate is for the supervisor to schedule employee feedback sessions during times in which the supervisor and the employee can chat about work (Halloran and Frunzi, 1986). Sometimes the best forms of supervision occur during downtime and off-the-job (what the Disney Corporation refers to as "off stage"). Regardless, supervision should be a balanced system of scheduled and unscheduled interactions with employees. The formal, structured meetings provide the framework for fostering human relations, clarifying role expectations, and assessing job performance. The unstructured setting allow workers and the supervisor to come together in real time to deal with more immediate on-the-job problems.

Teams: Staff and Supervisors Working Toward Common Goals

Supervision does not occur in a vacuum. Given our earlier discussions, the supervisor's most fundamental job is to mold an effective work team which has clearly defined, familiar goals (Tubbs, 1984). Therefore, it is important for supervisors to recognize the fact that they are not managing individual employees and their specific tasks, but that they are managing the process in which these individuals interact in order to accomplish departmental objectives.

In terms of developing team spirit and camaraderie, supervisors can use a tactic of being both seen and heard. They create the culture and climate of the work environment through their activities, and because of this need to set the proper tone for how the work setting functions. This is particularly true in an administrative academic environment where many employees have chosen to work (usually for less pay) in a college or university because they perceive the college setting as a friendlier environment than business.

For example, if supervisors want to have a friendly and warm work environment then they must exhibit those behaviors that would encourage friendly and warm responses from their employees. Cultural differences aside, saying "good morning," briefly asking about their employees' weekend, sharing a few jokes, noticing a new suit or haircut, asking about their employees' families -- all of these things add to a personalized and respectful environment in the workplace. From our perspective, college should not only be a fun and educational place for the students but for the staff and everyone else that works there as well.

Should a Supervisor Worry About Being Liked?

In the Theory X approach, whether or not a supervisor is liked is hardly the issue (McGregor, 1960). Here, making sure the job gets done and the governing authorities get what they have mandated is clearly superior to feelings or relationships. The job is what is important, and getting the job done is the only thing supervisors in this type of environment would every worry about. In a way, this is the easy approach to implement. Supervisors don't have to worry about whether or not subordinates like them. Supervisors only have to worry about meeting the expectations of their own superiors.

There are other opinions. In a line contributed to Machiavelli in *The Prince* (Donno, 1966), he states that in a superior-subordinate relationship, it is better to be respected and feared than to be liked. His reasoning goes on to state that in times of crisis, one cannot trust a relationship where friendship or even love define them. Rather, if a subordinate is truly fearful of the superior, then when the superior gives a directive, the subordinate carries it out in order to avoid negative consequences. Machiavelli advocated that this was by far the better circumstance for assuring that what the superior felt needed to get done would get done.

Unfortunately, the Machiavellian approach is alive and well in many management circles, including college and university campuses. Often, environments that are strained through crisis, or steeped in particular traditions, or led by highly authoritarian leaders all tend to develop cultures where fear rules and friendships are regarded as potential palace coups.

As it turns out, Machiavelli was incorrect, particularly if he were framing managerial theory for modern day organizations and campuses. Because of our growing understanding and appreciation for the human resource approach to effective supervision, it is important to understand that people work better in a supportive and motivational environment than they do in an authoritarian and punitive environment (Likert, 1967).

This is the issue of understanding the benefits of motivation over the benefits of force. In a motivational environment, people are not only happier to be there, they are usually far more productive. Not only that, their production is usually of a very high quality. In contrast, in an authoritarian and punitive environment, people will most likely do the minimum to meet expectations. Going the extra mile is out of the question, to say nothing about any expectations for higher levels of quality or innovation.

The bottom line is that supervisors need to create a friendly environment where people want to go to work and do their work to achieve pride and satisfaction. There is no way this can be accomplished if subordinates do not like or if they fear their supervisors.

To what extent, then, should supervisors worry about being liked? Are there limits? To reply to these questions, we once again refer to some of the lessons of the PAC model. Honesty, objectivity, and trust between a supervisor and an employee (or group of employees) should engender a healthy respect for each other in the work place. This may or may not lead to after-hour social friendships, but then again, it is always incorrect for organizations (including colleges and universities) to infringe on the personal and private rights of its employees. A supervisor's concern here needs to be for the relationships that occur in the work place and for those relationships which are friendly, professional, objective, and job-oriented will always prove to be the most beneficial to the people involved as well as to the campus they serve. Adult-adult working relationships lead to optimal work outcomes. Treating each other with respect always brings out the best of the human resource.

We offer one final thought. One major differentiator between supervisors and subordinates is that of power (Brown, 1983). Power is one of the great rewards of becoming a supervisor and this reward increases as one moves up the managerial ladder. In this discussion, it is important that supervisors recognize that because of power, they have special responsibilities in regard to building effective working relationships with employees. First, supervisors are in the greater position to impact the relationship because of their position power. Second, supervisors should never abuse position power to take advantage of a situation or of an employee. Third, leadership is a special kind of personal power, which suggests that most subordinates will look toward their supervisors to determine the nature of any developing relationship. Finally, fourth, power is a resource – a resource entrusted to supervisors to be of benefit to the campus. Supervisors must respect their power and use it properly in an honest and objective attempt to do the best job possible for the college or university.

ಸು Chapter 4 ಞ

Strategies for Problem Solving

Wouldn't it be great if everything worked out the way it is supposed to? Wouldn't it make life much easier if the plans we made worked out to the exact conclusions that we were hoping for? Wouldn't it be wonderful if nothing ever went wrong? To which we might add, what would it be like to live in a perfect world?

Of course, we don't live in a perfect world, and interestingly enough, if we all did live in a perfect world, there would be no need for managers! In a perfect world, everyone would know what they needed to do, would do it, and be able to solve any and all problems on their own. But since the world we inhabit is highly imperfect, subject to increasing and dramatic changes, and fraught with the unknown, there will always be problems, and there will always be a need for good managers. Of the duties of a supervisor, problem solving is perhaps the greatest single responsibility that any manager faces, and how she/he conducts problem solving will absolutely determine that manager's or supervisor's level of effectiveness (Simon, 1976).

This is clearly true in today's colleges and universities. Resources are scarce; good people are hard to find; students are becoming more activist in their education; providers of grants and contracts want more accountability; states are becoming more active in the operations of their state-supported colleges and universities; and quantum change is the name of the game. In this complex world, things go wrong. If this isn't bad enough, things go wrong randomly and on a range of severity from just a little bit wrong to a whole lot wrong.

Assigning blame is a human activity. Partially because it is safer not to be the cause of problems, but also because of our up bringing, someone has to take the heat when things go wrong. However, as we have seen in our discussion of the PAC model, there are choices regarding how individual respond when facing problems: objectively, in looking for the root causes of problems and the best possible remedies; and emotionally, where anger clouds the issues and child-like or parent-like predispositions take over and solutions are more punitive than corrective.

Who is to Blame When Things Go Wrong?

Whenever things go wrong, there is a natural tendency to want to know why. Often, people look for the human causes because unpredictable behavior can lead to unintended results. Technology can also be the culprit as computers go down, or phone lines get jammed, or other office equipment breaks down. Too, some look to the unexplainable and tell us that, "It's God's will." Regardless, when things go wrong, they have to be fixed, and supervisors are always the first line of responsibility for determining that something has gone wrong, how it can be fixed, who or what caused it, and how can they insure that the problems will not recur.

For supervisors, then, this question always has the same response – supervisors are to blame, at least in the sense that they are responsible. Responsibility comes with the job, and whether or not the individual is personally responsible for the problem, it doesn't matter. The authority that the organization has given to the supervisor to manage its human resources brings with it the responsibility to account for whatever happens within the supervisor's area of responsibility.

This said, then the next issue is what actually caused the problem. Supervisors are responsible for overseeing much of the work that is done, not for doing the work. Certainly, if the reality is that one of the supervisor's subordinates has caused a problem, the supervisor must be able to establish this as fact. Then, the supervisor is faced with a choice – how to react and respond. In making a choice, the supervisor must realize that he/she must engage in some corrective action, but again, there is a choice in terms of what form that corrective action should take. One choice is the parental choice: make sure that the offender realizes the implications of the problem she/he has caused; take punitive actions; and then make sure that the offender fully understands that this type of mistake (or purposeful act) will not be tolerated in the future. The second choice is the adult choice: discover what caused the problem (misinformation, confusion, poor judgment, or whatever); discover the best remedy for the problem; and then work with the employees to make sure the problem does not reoccur (training, counseling, improving lines of communication, or what else might be useful). As you might expect, the authors of this book believe that the second approach is the best, and will lead to optimal problem-solving outcomes for everyone involved (Elbing, 1970).

We also do not want to suggest here that the result of all problem solving will be improved performance by all concerned. If the problem is an employee who simply does not or cannot meet expectations, it could well mean that the supervisor is going to follow campus guidelines to transfer out the problem employee or let that person go. These are hard choices, but from an objective point of view, the overriding interests here are those of the department, the division, and the campus as a whole. By not dealing objectively with a problem employee (allowing the problem to continue or even get worse) supervisors must take responsibility for their actions and bear the blame for lower levels of expected performance. In the long run, no one wins here, everyone is damaged, and the institution suffers. The key is objectivity.

A Major Part of Supervision Responsibility

As we stated above, part of what supervisors must fully understand is that they are responsible for whatever happens within the department. In colleges and universities, this means that for a department chair, what happens in the classroom is ultimately her/his responsibility.

For academic supervisors, tenure presents the potential for limited actions when working with a tenured professor who isn't performing well in the classroom (or as a researcher or service provider). It's important to remember, however, that tenure isn't something that faculty want in place to protect them from the consequences of their own failings. It is in place to assure academic freedom, and nothing in the concept of tenure suggests anything else. Therefore, while tenure might make the process of reforming or removing a professor an elongated process, it doesn't mean that department chairs and deans cannot do everything in their power to help assure the highest levels of quality in their departments, schools, or colleges. In no way does the presence of tenure alter the demands of responsibility (Lewis and Smith, 1994).

Beyond academic supervision, tenure is not an issue, though unionism may be. Non-academic supervisory responsibilities throughout the campus are very similar to those of traditional business firms as well as not-for-profit and governmental agencies. Here, the staff is year-round (compared to academics who might have more of a 9-month schedule) and they perform support activities for the organization very much like any other organization. Supervisory responsibility may be partially defined by union rules, state personnel system rules, campus policies and procedures, and tradition. In these settings, it is crucial that supervisors determine what these various sets of rules determine to be acceptable problem-solving activities and then still remember that regardless, they is still in charge of the work group and what ever goes wrong, they are still responsible.

If Things Go Wrong, Don't Worry About Finding the Scapegoat

Scapegoats are wonderful. When a problem can be attributed to a particular person, that person must shoulder the blame and pay the consequences. This is excellent news for everyone else who find themselves in the situation – the heat is on the scapegoat and off everyone else.

There are several problems with scapegoating, including that the accused person may or may not be guilty. Even so, if the person is responsible for the problem, this is a past event. The bigger issue is remedying the problem and getting back to normal operation. So rather than seeking someone to blame, an effective supervisor will concentrate more on fixing the problem. Then, once the problem has been mitigated, the supervisor can seek the true cause of the problem (hopefully in a calm and objective atmosphere), isolate the root of the problem and then fix it.

Getting On With It

As we stated earlier, organizational learning is an important process in all organizations and individuals throughout the organization learn from their successes and mistakes. Over-reaction to problems can stunt this learning process and certainly emotional over-reaction will take learning in the wrong direction. It tends to give out the message that the organization really does not want to tolerate innovation and creativity, and that the way to survive is to just do the job (not necessarily well, just get it done) (Wick & Leon, 1993). An unemotional process of problem solving adds to organizational learning. This means that as the college or university continues its journey, it continuously equips itself with new ideas and tools that help it compete more effectively in the academic community. In this sense, problems serve a valuable service by helping the campus learn more about itself and developing procedures that will help it run more smoothly in the future; and if the process has been truly unemotional, the lessons are positive, not punitive. We do not suggest here that problems are good, just that they can be helpful if dealt with properly.

This is why blame isn't really helpful. It tends to draw the process away from problem solving and organizational learning and focusing on finding someone to punish. Instead, when one remembers that college and university campuses are human organizations, one must also remember that problems are inevitable. Being prepared for problems and solving them quickly and objectively are two marks of an outstanding supervisor.

What About Potential Bad Feelings?

It's a rather common occurrence that people don't like their bosses. Some of this is rational and some of it is not. From a rational point of view, the supervisor controls resources and makes decisions about those resources that affect others. Those others may or may not like the decisions that are made and can form a dislike for the decision-maker as well. In an era of squeezed resources, managers and supervisors make hard decisions, including employee scale-back and cutback decisions, and it is not reasonable to assume everyone is going to be happy with those decisions.

The irrational point of view comes from human nature. We are all parochial animals, who look out for ourselves and those we love first and foremost. Sometimes this element of self-worth gets out of perspective and some people begin to allow emotions, prejudices, and fears to influence their behavior. This can happen when one person is put in charge of another person or a group. Emotions, prejudices, and fears can place the new supervisor in a precarious position just by virtue of being appointed to the position. Unlike the rational issues above, the supervisor's responsibility becomes much more tricky and challenging when irrational factors are also at play (Aronson, 1980).

So, what if nobody likes you? If a supervisor needs friendship above the satisfaction of doing the job well, then perhaps this person should not be in the position. If a supervisor is concerned with doing her or his best to support the college or university, then being liked isn't quite so important (McClelland, 1966). The good news is that, over time, an effective supervisor can make this issue simply go away using some of the tactics below.

Ultimately It's an Issue of Trust and Integrity

No one has said throughout this book that supervision is easy. Many times it's not. Both authors have heard many colleagues say it and have said it themselves – being a supervisor sometimes isn't any fun. Yet, this important position is crucial to the overall activities of the campus. While the position can be extremely rewarding, particularly after a job has been done well, it's not child's play. It is a responsible position that requires the highest amount of ethical standards and personal integrity.

Make Sure This Applies to You. Supervisors are faced with many ambiguous situations and must make choices. Some choices are convenient and easy (like finding and punishing a scapegoat as we discussed above). Other choices are hard to make and difficult to implement. The decision rule, however, should always be that of doing what is best for the entire college or university and doing it in the most ethical and humane manner possible.

Unfortunately, there is no guidebook for every situation (if X happens, then apply remedy C). Instead, each situation tends to be unique and calls on the supervisor to come up with a new approach or a new solution. Discussion with peers can be helpful, and certainly knowing the rules of the game are imperative, but often it comes down to a supervisor making her or his own final decision. Being able to test that decision against the above decision rule at least assures that the manager will make as optimal decision as he or she was able to do, and there's nothing wrong with that (McFarland, 1986).

What About Subordinate Ethics? While it is critical that a manager or supervisor act with only the highest level of ethics and personal integrity, it is also important that each and every subordinate do the same. The role of the supervisor as leader is an important understanding in that a leader can effectively influence the behavior of followers. In this case, a supervisor who is ethical and demands ethical practices of subordinates practically has the job complete. Too, enforcing the adult-to-adult relationship will mean that the supervisor should be effective in deterring unethical behaviors.

If subordinates refuse to act ethically and responsibly, then, it is entirely appropriate to consider replacing them. While both authors feel that it is always important to save a campus's valuable human resources, they also recognize the reality that some people can't be saved. Acting in an unethical manner is always a cause for corrective action, and if that corrective action is not effective, then supervisors must not be afraid to recommend dismissal. Having and tolerating an employee who does not work for the overall good of the campus is a clear blemish on the character and credibility of the supervisor. An effective supervisor will not tolerate this.

It is important that all supervisors work hard to build trust, objectivity, and mutual understanding as the hallmarks of how they work with subordinates on a daily basis. As we have point out earlier, trust is a difficult commodity to attain and maintain, and once it has been destroyed, it is nearly impossible to rebuild it. Acting unethically destroys trust, not only with subordinates, but with peers and managers as well. Acting ethically, objectively, and humanely in every situation is the most effective way of building and sustaining the trust which each supervisor must rely on to be successful in the position.

Ultimately it's an Issue of Achieving Organizational Goals

Problems, successes, challenges, and relationships are all part of the job of a supervisor. The day-to-day pressures of dealing with these realities often obscure the purpose of being there in the first place. This is a condition that supervisors must guard against. While strategic management is conducted at the highest levels of the campus, and focuses on the overall activities that will provide long-term health and success for the college or university, managers and supervisors throughout the campus have the awesome responsibility of carrying out the strategic plan. They do this on the functional level (Coulter, 2002). The relationship between campus-wide strategy and functional level operations should always be apparent in the activities of supervisors as they oversee their departments and human resources for which they are responsible. Acting within this framework, supervisors implement their college or university strategic plan on a day-to-day basis. Recognizing this relationship as part of a supervisor's job is one of the most exciting and fulfilling elements of the job.

To summarize, a supervisor can be effective in working with subordinates objectively by:
> Appealing to what is best for the organization,
> Being willing to negotiate conditions, and
> By listening and analyzing before acting.

One More Time - the Adult-Adult Relationship

Problem solving is one of the most severe of challenges to the PAC model. It is so easy to slip back into the parental role (supervisor) and the child role (subordinates) when the status quo is breached and a problem is apparent. From tradition, people slip easily into emotional states and with the position power of supervisors, it is easy for these roles to emerge.

Yet, as one recognizes that good can come from problem solving (organizational learning), and resisting the natural tendency to revert to parent-child roles, supervisors need to control the situation and enforce the adult-adult approach. Developing a win-win atmosphere allows everyone to use problem solving as one method of developing better and more effective operating methods. This is true in the academic side of the house just as it is in the support side of the campus.

How Does One Effectively Deal with One's Problem Employees?

One would like to think that, like Douglas McGregor's (1960) Theory Y manager's assumptions, in an academic setting employees and faculty truly behave as if work was as natural as play and that employees see their work as the primary motivating factor for their performance. Experience, however, has shown us that in spite of an academic settings (and some people in the field might say that due to the academic setting), administrative employees and faculty can and do become problem children for first-line supervisors.

Definition

Timm (1984) has suggested that problem employees in an academic context are those employees who continually perform poorly on the job and/or who interrupt and/or hinder the work of others. Specifically, problem employees resist rules and authority, (Etzioni, 1964) oppose change (French and Bell, 1995), are maladjusted to their work environment (Timm and Peterson, 1982), act immaturely (assume the child role) (Argyris, 1962), and negatively impact both the culture of the organization and the specific work group that they are a member of (Dyer, 1977; Tubbs, 1978). Putting it bluntly, problem workers act like cancer cells in an organism. They not infect only the surrounding cells (individuals) but may contaminate other vital organs (parts of the organization). Problem employees sew the seeds of discord and flame the fires of discontent.

Causes

Workers are not born disgruntled and certainly do not exhibit malcontented behavior when first hired by the institution. It is quite possible that the employee recruitment and selection process may not be able to weed out problem workers (Ivanevich, 2001). Usually employees are quite committed to their jobs during their probationary period (usually three to six months for administrative employees, and four to seven years for faculty) and will continue to be at least compliant well after their trial period (Kopelman, 1986). The real question, then, is what has happened after this tryout period to change the employees' performance?

Usually an employee's work deteriorates due to individual, organizational, environmental and job factors related to the employee's work environment (Griffin, 1982). Figure 4-1, below, identifies these factors.

Figure 4-1
FACTORS AFFECTING EMPLOYEE PERFORMANCE

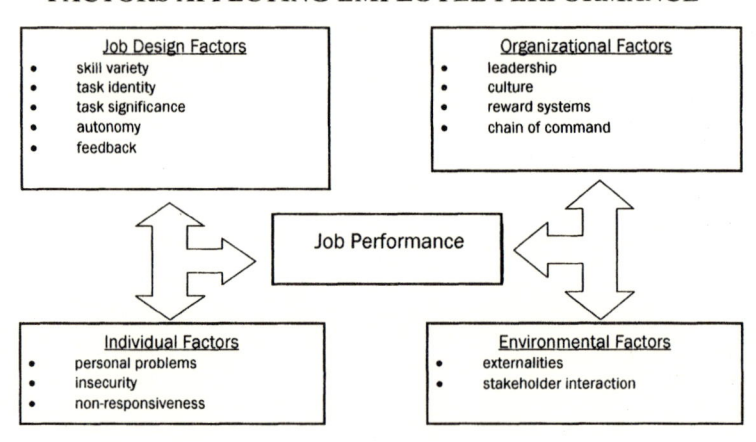

Job Design Factors
- skill variety
- task identity
- task significance
- autonomy
- feedback

Organizational Factors
- leadership
- culture
- reward systems
- chain of command

Job Performance

Individual Factors
- personal problems
- insecurity
- non-responsiveness

Environmental Factors
- externalities
- stakeholder interaction

Individual Factors. The three individual factors include personal problems, insensitivity to other employees' needs, and non-responsiveness to performance feedback (Timm, 1984). In terms of *personal problems*, it is very difficult to expect employees to separate their personal life from his or her work life since people define who they are by what they do and where they work (Whyte, 1956; Kaufman, 1969). Critical events in a person's family life (death of a loved one, divorce, legal and/or financial difficulties, poor health, drug and/or alcohol abuse, among others) cannot help but impact on-the-job performance and therefore supervisors should expect employees' behavior to correlate to such critical incidents.

Insensitivity to others' needs (a lack of empathy) denotes an intolerance and dehumanization of others and the rationalization of harmful or inappropriate acts (i.e. aggression, prejudice, spite, etc...) (Aronson, 1980). In many cases, these individuals are not aware of their own lack of empathy (or the appearance therein) and merely have to have associated incidents pointed out to them in order to heighten their awareness of the problem. Once they are aware of the impact of their behavior on others, they will cease said actions (Luft, 1961). On the other hand, other employees may be aware of the situation they are creating but truly devalue their fellow workers. They see no problem in their dehumanizing actions (yelling, threatening, or criticizing others publicly) since they tend to be narcissistic and self-serving.

When employees ignore supervisors' suggestions or refuse to change their work habits in order to meet performance standards, their behavior is categorized as *non-responsive*. Whether due to lack of work motivation, sheer stubbornness, or the desire to act in a deviant manner, these employees disregard both formal and informal performance evaluations. It doesn't matter if these employees don't care about their job performance, whether they think they know the best way do to something, or are actually out to sabotage the institution, their performance is substandard and needs to be dealt with.

Organizational Factors. Employees can also become problems when features of the organization (leadership, culture, reward systems, chain of command) create a misfit between employees and their jobs. *Leadership*, whether of the particular work group or the organization in general, plays a role in aggravating the problem worker through the style of leadership employed, the message or vision the leader conveys (and the resultant college *culture* created from that style and vision), and the equity of treatment (Lussier and Achua, 2001).

In terms of leadership style, most employees in an academic setting (especially faculty) react very poorly to autocratic styles of leadership, even a benevolent autocrat (Bennis, 1989). Employees wish to be asked, not told; consulted, not cajoled; and treated like adults, not as children. Subordinates want to feel that they have rights as well as responsibilities in their organization and that their opinions are valued. When supervisors diminish an employee's self-worth through directive, rather than supportive, leadership, they not only lose the work effort of that employee but have sewn the seeds for the destruction of their operating unit.

We are not arguing that at times a strong leadership position is not warranted. On the contrary, literature in the field has identified the need for a contingency style of leadership, one that changes to fit the particular work situation (Yukl, 1994). What we are saying, however, is that situations that call for this style of supervising, especially in academic settings, is not the norm but the exception to the norm. Hersey and Blanchard (1993) have suggested that there may well be two specific situations warrant an autocratic style of leadership:

1. Self-direction and consultation have failed and the employee is resistant to taking responsibility for the situation.
2. Emergency situations requiring immediate and decisive actions (for example, there are sharp drops in enrollment, the local area network goes off-line, the faculty or staff go on a wild cat strike, or the like).

If some leadership styles define the transactions between employee and supervisor, then other styles define the vision or mission underlying the message behind those transactions. For many employees, their supervisor represents the organization - its values, norms, and belief systems. It is important that supervisors pay attention to the messages embedded in their interactions with employees to ensure that the message they convey to their employees about the values of the organization are consistent with the institution's ideals and match the morals of their employees (McFarland, 1986).

Employees will treat students (the college's consumers) the same way that their supervisors treat them. They will enact the values to which they themselves have been exposed to. For example, a college or university that espouses a warm and friendly environment (students go there for the family feel of the college) must institutionalize that culture by having administrative and faculty supervisors treat their employees in like manner.

Equity of treatment is of crucial consequence as a norm or value of the organization. Several theories of worker motivation (Steers, Porter and Bigley, 1996) have indicated that employees who believe that they are receiving unfair treatment from their supervisors will reduce both their productivity and the quality of their work. Supervisors must become acutely aware not only of how they treat their employees but also of the perception of other employees in their unit of that fairness. Employees compare their perception of how others are treated by their supervisor to the treatment they themselves receive in order to determine the relative equity of the situation (Adams, 1965).

We are not suggesting that employees must receive the same treatment since each employee has different needs and different capabilities. In fact, we recognize that issues such as seniority and tenure may make it impossible to do so. What we are suggesting, however, is that equitable or fair treatment requires that the supervisor act as impartially as possible, rely on facts (not rumors), and that benefits employees derive from their status (seniority, for example) be balanced with opportunities for other employees to obtain that status (Rawls, 1971).

Created through college leadership and tradition, *culture* can certainly create problem employees when the employees' values are not attuned to that of the organization's. For example, the emergence of proprietary and in particular corporate colleges and universities has created a new role for faculty in these alternative academic settings - that of a non-tenurable employee. Since these universities are not as interested in knowledge creation, but rather in knowledge transference, the customs and ceremonies surrounding faculty research have been eliminated (Rowley and Sherman, 2001). Traditional faculty fair poorly in these settings since their expectations for relatively higher status in this culture are not warranted. This discussion can be continued when examining the relative orientation of traditional institutions and its faculty towards research.

From a supervisor's perspective, culture includes patterns of behavior, norms, values and basic assumptions that underlie the work environment (Ott, 1989). More specifically, the culture of the work unit determines the right and wrong way to do things as well as the right and wrong way to think about the unit and the organization. Problem employees arise when the employee continues to be in the wrong and has not altered his or her behavior to be more aligned with cultural norms. For example, one of the authors works in an institution where the dress norms of the faculty are very relaxed (especially in the summer). When he continued to come to work in a suit and tie, he received flippant comments from some of the senior faculty on campus and even a rather poignant remark from the university president. This author has now slightly modified his attire (sports jacket versus suit) and seems to have accommodated the culture. The key issue for supervisors is to create and nurture a culture within his or her operating unit that reinforces positive individual employee and group performance and then to adapt to them themselves.

Rewards systems, both formal and informal, also impact employee performance and may be a lead to problem workers. Many of the formal reward systems are outside the supervisor's purview and further may have minimal connections to worker productivity (union contracts, campus-wide salary raises). These systems tend to reward longevity on the job over merit and therefore compensate non-job related factors. These systems may be perceived as inequitable to newer employees who feel that they should be recompensed based upon performance criteria. Therefore, supervisors need to discern what latitude they have (if any) in terms of the formal reward system.

Certain colleges do offer faculty and staff merit raises and the supervisor should be quite careful to connect compensation with performance using standardized performance appraisal and review systems (Carroll and Schneier, 1982). However, Steven Kerr (1975) cautioned supervisors that they should not hope for certain a type of behavior (such as quality teaching) if their institutional reward system is based upon criteria that do not include those behaviors (such as tenure and promotion based upon research standards).

Second, supervisors certainly can avail themselves of informal reward systems that may not be directly connected to compensation. Ironically, a compliment or a pat on the back, taking an office worker out to lunch, selecting the employee of the month, and other methods for acknowledging a job well done, costs the college minimal yet recognize and reinforce productive workers. Many employees become disgruntled because they feel that their supervisor has not personally recognized their good work.

The *organizational hierarchy*, or chain of command, may also have a negative impact on worker productivity. The governing body of the college determines the organization's overall structure, yet it is the supervisor's job to match his or her unit's internal structure to the external work environment (Lawrence and Lorsch, 1969).

Mintzberg (1979) described structures as highly formal/bureaucratic or highly informal/organic. According to Mintzberg, formalized structures are appropriate in very stable task environments -- the work is quite predictable, routine and produces specialists who become expert in their tasks. These structures tend to have many layers of management and very few employees per layer.

For example, in larger academic departments or divisions, there may be smaller subunits (such as a segment of the overall discipline – HRM as part of a management department) that allow for greater employee interaction and teamwork. This type of structuring would allow colleges to develop centers of excellence within a broader school or division structure and potentially create research teams. The challenge for supervisors then becomes that of coordinating the operations of these individual units so that they work as a whole while balancing the ability of the individuals in those specialized units to work interdependently (Galbraith, 1977).

On the other hand, organic structures work well in environments that are not as stable -- where work is unpredictable. Here, employees develop flexibility in order to constantly change and adapt to new circumstances. These structures tend to have very few layers of management, and many employees per layer.

In administrative units, merging separate but well connected units may enhance student service and worker productivity. Workers develop a broader array of skills aimed at dealing with a wider scope of operations. By trying to develop a one stop shop for service, the supervisor's challenge becomes ensuring that employees have access to all information they will need to be able to answer and resolve student problems (Galbraith, 1977).

Job Design Factors. Job-specific factors that may create problem employees include *skill variety, task identity, task significance, autonomy, and job feedback* (Hackman and Oldham, 1980). *Skill variety*, the variance in actual tasks to be completed; *task identity*, the ability of the employee to clearly know the tasks to be performed; and *task significance*, the importance of the task in the completion of the overall product or service, all directly impact the meaningfulness of the work experience. Jobs that are designed with large skill variety, high task identity, and high task significance produce high employee motivation -- the employee values his or her work and is driven to complete its tasks.

Another concern is that certain jobs are innately more meaningful than others. Most faculty are highly motivated instructors and researchers given the array of responsibilities, their personal identification with the job, and their perceived importance of the task. This may differ dramatically from the department secretary's position that may have more routine tasks, and be perceived as having less direct impact on students. One of the authors must admit that this was the reason that he went through four secretaries in four years. His expectations were that the secretary of the department would be as committed to her job to the extent that he and the rest of the faculty were to theirs. Upon questioning the reasons for quitting their jobs, the secretaries stated that they did not see the importance of their work and did not want to work in an environment where their job was a career.

Supervisors, however, do have the power to make jobs more meaningful. Combining tasks and establishing client relations can increase skill variety. Task identity enlarges jobs through combining tasks and forming natural work units. Finally, the forming of natural work units significantly enhances task significance (Kopelman, 1986). Again, supervisors can raise the level of meaningfulness to meet employee needs while not simply giving workers more to do.

Autonomy in a job is the relative freedom the employee experiences in terms of performing his or her work functions. Supervisors can increase their employees' on-the-job autonomy through job enrichment and greater student interface and will result in employees feeling more responsible for their performance outcomes (Pinder, 1984).

In the case of supervising faculty, they have immense autonomy in that they decide not only their instructional method and their textbooks but also may choose the courses they teach and when their classes are to be held. They have a high level of interaction with students and may increase these interactions through participation in extra-curricula activities.

Non-academic supervisors in an academic environment may not have it as easy as their academic counterparts in that clerical positions tend to have fixed hours and duties with interdependent tasks. Even so, technology has provided the opportunity for greater autonomy in many of these positions since an individual can process work instantaneously and from anywhere that has access to the web and a telephone (Ronen, 1981).

Going back to the example of the four department secretaries, one of the reasons that they may have transferred from their position is that they may not have wanted the accountability associated with a more autonomous job. Some employees are quite happy just doing what they are told to do, and supervisors need to work with employees to discover how much responsibility they are actually willing to accept. It was clear to the author in question that he had greater expectations for this position when, in describing its duties and functions, an applicant remarked "are you sure that this is a secretary's job?"

Last, *feedback* provides employees with knowledge concerning their actual performance, thereby impacting both employee satisfaction and organizational commitment (Kopelman, 1986). Interestingly enough, the literature is not clear on whether happy workers are always productive workers (Steers, Porter and Bigley, 1996), but the literature is certainly clear on the impact of feedback on productivity -- the more information that workers have on their performance, the greater the probability that they will enhance that performance (Wren, 1994). From a total quality management perspective, mutual feedback and close interaction of departments is an elementary aspect of a productive organization (Lewis and Smith, 1994).

Environmental Factors. Externalities are any factors in the operating environment of the college or university that may directly impact the organization and employees' job design. These are the *political, economic, social,* and *technological* trends that impact all organizations – some management strategists warmly refer to them as "P.E.S.T.s". Thompson (1967) argued that it is the job of supervisors and their staffs to protect the technical core, or the on-the-job workers, from interference from externalities that hinder task performance. Our best example is the model of academic department secretary who functions as guardian of the faculty -- no one sees faculty without an appointment, no interrupting phone calls to disturb their thoughts. This guarding-type of activity provides the time and freedom for faculty members to pursue their research and develop their courses in the sanctity of their offices or even better, their homes.

Interacting with organizational stakeholders can also create problem employees. Over the years, we have heard several faculty and administrative personnel lament dealings with students and their parents, alumni, members of the Board of Trustees, government and regulatory agencies, lending institutions, major suppliers, and the general public. Like De Tocqueville in his discussion on democracy, they mourn the death of the imperial university and rue the day in which a college education became a commodity; a mere good to be exploited by both the buyer (the student) and the seller (the college or university).

It is true that colleges and universities do not have a long history of being customer-oriented (Rowley and Sherman, 2001). Only in the last decade or two of the 21st century have some small and comprehensive colleges and universities embraced the notion that their job was not primarily knowledge creation (research) but rather knowledge dissemination (teaching). These changes have been driven by the development of alternative college education delivery systems, most notably education through the Internet, and the lack of resources necessary to create research centers of excellence. Some campuses are beginning to understand the need to compete for students not only through the more traditional methods of scholarships and program marketing, but rather through the delivery of high quality services which add value to a student's college experience. In interacting with the external interest groups, therefore, college employees will find the traditional bureaucratic model of behavior unacceptable by both their superiors and the college's stakeholders.

Categories of Difficult Employees

When examining the factors that impact employee performance, Ivancevich (2001) has identified four groupings or specific sources based upon those factors:
1. Employees whose work is below standards due to lack of abilities, training, or drive -- individual, job design, and organizational factors.
2. Employees who consistently break company rules and do not respond to supervisory correction -- individual and organizational factors.

3. Employees whose off the job personal problems affect their on the job performance -- individual and environmental factors.
4. Employees who violate the law on-the-job -- environmental factors.

Dealing With Problem Employees: Rehabilitate, Relocate, Demote and Remove

In dealing with problems employees, the remedies employed should be progressive in nature and determined by the ability of the employee to alter his or her negative performance.

Rehabilitation. The least progressive intervention, is nonetheless a rather appealing term to use for the first method of dealing with problem employees. It suggests that the employees' actions were inappropriate and that they need to change the behaviors that led up to poor job performance. The key to rehabilitation is understanding that poor job performance is an antecedent or result of a series of on-the-job and off-the-job behaviors (Luthans, 1998).

In order to become rehabilitated, the employees must first recognize and accept the fact that their performance is unacceptable. The supervisor must therefore be able to confront the employee in question with the problem and work with the employee to develop a solution strategy.

Timm (1984) encourages supervisors to gather information about the problem, more specifically documented evidence or examples of poor work habits (such as absenteeism, lateness, low productivity, missed deadlines, etc.); review the employee's entire record; consider the specific circumstances leading to the poor performance (looking at the personal, job design, organizational, and environmental factors); check the consistency of the poor work behavior; check to make sure that there are no legal and contractual restrictions on solving the problem; and remain objective. Burack and Smith (1977) noted that once the supervisor is ready to confront the problem employee, the supervisor needs to: a) promptly discuss the situation in private; b) treat his or her actions as corrective, not punitive; c) avoid sarcasm, threats, argue or show anger; d) criticize the behavior, not the employee; e) impose any disciplinary measures as prescribed by work rules and as fits the infraction; and f) follow-up meeting with continued formal and informal feedback on job performance.

Morrison and O'Hearne (1977) employed a practical transactional analysis approach in handling problem employees and suggested offering criticism that will be instructive and improve job performance. They specifically recommended constructive criticism using a situational description that focused upon the causes and the effects of the poor performance. Regardless of the specific method, the key in confrontation is helping the employee first determine the category or sources of the problem, and then taking action specifically geared toward solving it.

For example, in the case of an employee whose work performance is poor due to lack of training, motivation and ability, the supervisor needs to determine in which areas the problem is occurring and what if any corrective actions can be taken. If the problem is due to off-the-job factors, such as alcohol and drug abuse, the supervisor may refer employees to an Employee Assistance Program (EAP) for external rehabilitation. Theft or other illegal acts may also lead to criminal rehabilitation while persistent rule violators may obtain psychological counseling (Ivancevich, 2001).

Relocation/Demotion. It is also quite possible that an employee and the supervisor either cannot reach an agreement on how to solve the employee's performance problem or agree that the employee is not capable of performing his or her current job at an acceptable level. A job transfer may provide the employee a real second chance and allow him or her to try another job, at a similar level of difficulty, that may better address their needs. In some cases a demotion is also in order either because of legal/union issues, as a recognition of continued rule-breaking, or the employee was underqualified for their last position. Demotions, however, tend to have a very negative motivating effect and may be offered as an expedient method for phasing out an employee.

Removal. Dismissing an employee is truly the final solution in the sense that the supervisor and the organization have given up on trying to salvage the employee's job performance and feels that no other alternative is available. Firing an employee, for some colleges and universities, may be a very difficult process given the presence of union shops and formalized grievance procedures. However, certain actions by an employee may lead to immediate dismissal such as theft, physical violence, and insubordination. Other types of behavior such as incompetence and poor attitude may be less clear-cut and supervisors tread on thin ice when seeking to dismiss individuals who fit these categories. Regardless of the reason for letting an employee go, supervisors should have strong documentation for such an action and be able to demonstrate that less stringent, alternative measures were tried prior to this action or that the action taken, according to college policy, results in immediate expulsion.

Behavioral Types of Difficult People

Housel (2002) suggested that another interesting alternative approach to analyzing the cause(s) of a problem employee is to study the behavioral styles exhibited by these workers. He suggested that six styles or types exist:
- Controlling aggressors = act openly hostile and negative.

- Volcanoes = unpredictable and volatile.
- Passive-aggressors = non-confrontational; use subtle subversive tactics.
- Constant complainers = whiners; find fault in everything.
- Slackers = non-contributors; never meet deadlines.
- Oppositional defiants = contradictory; thrive on controversy.

Note that we can go back to transactional analysis (TA) to explain these behavioral types. Employees acting in an aggressive, overt manner (controlling aggressors and perhaps volcanoes) are enacting the parent role by trying to impose their will upon the situation. They are attempting to bully or cajole their supervisors and fellow employees into accepting their authority (asking these individuals to adopt the child role). In an academic workplace, faculty may employ their expert status in their field in order to achieve this effect while nonacademic employees may refer to either their own administrative expertise or their seniority status.

The child role is enacted by employees when individuals either openly defy authority (oppositional defiants), try to subvert authority (passive-aggressors and slackers), or just carp about authority (constant complainers). Usually these behaviors are exhibited when faculty and staff feel powerless to change their work environment and/or feel that a work situation is inequitable. Timm (1984) further commented that people like to test the "limits of acceptable behavior" (p. 411) and used the analogy of a small child acting out poor behavior to test his or her parents' tolerance. He cautioned supervisors to overcome their tendency not to set and enforce boundaries, and we would add for only those employees who need to have them set for them, since restrictions reduce task ambiguity and uncertainty (Galbraith, 1977).

Housel (2002) also suggested several coping strategies in dealing with difficult people including: remaining calm, being patient, remaining in control of your own behavior, modeling desired behavior, paying attention to nonverbal cues, remembering to praise others, and being an active listener. Most importantly, Housel noted that supervisors should remember that they cannot change others' behaviors, just their own, and that good humor makes all things tolerable.

We would reinterpret Housel's suggestions, using TA, as recommending that supervisors enact the adult role with any difficult employee. Employees do put pressure on their supervisors, through the roles they enact, to assume a complimentary role. Although the complimentary transaction will result in reduced conflict, it will not solve the problem of reduced employee performance.

When in Doubt, Seek the Advice of Others

Most colleges and universities also have personnel handbooks and/or union contracts that detail the procedures that supervisors must follow in order to handle a particular personnel problem. However, policies and rules cannot cover every contingency and may be difficult to apply in certain situations. So when the procedure isn't clear, what is a supervisor to do?

Many department chairs and administrative supervisors may feel that when dealing with problem employees they live lonely lives of desperation. Both of the authors have served as department chairs and academic administrators and would note that we ourselves have been reticent in seeking the advice and counsel of others since we were under the false impression that we should have all the answers to all of our problems.

Misery does love company and we have found from our experiences that a wealth of knowledge and support can be accumulated through consultation with your immediate subordinates, your colleagues, and your superiors. Galbraith (1977) observed that seeking advice from co-workers and superiors is a very common method for reducing task uncertainty. This is especially appropriate when a supervisor is going to take dire measures in dealing with problem employees, such as demotion or removal.

Second, consultation makes excellence sense since there are usually legal ramifications in any punitive process. For example, although the doctrine of employment-at-will assumes that the employee and employer may terminate employment at any time, many state courts have taken a broad view of wrongful discharge. In Texas, employees cannot be discharged for refusing to break the law; in California, courts have found implied contracts disallowing discharge without cause based upon seniority, oral and written personnel policies; in Alaska, plaintiffs are allowed to sue in tort as well as contract based upon the good faith and fair dealing doctrine (Walsh and Schwartz, 1996).

Know When to Stop Trying to Solve Problems, Solve Them, and Move On

Most supervisors don't realize that most of their problem solving occurs at once, the moment the problem arises. Given the repetitive nature of the work they direct, most decisions that supervisors make are fairly routine or programmed (meaning that they occur on a scheduled basis such as class scheduling, dormitory assignments) and do not require a lot of thought and creativity. Immediacy of problem solving is critical to the success of their unit's operation - the problem needs to be solved and it needs to be solved now.

However, some situations, especially those dealing with problem employees, create internal conflicts for the supervisor and are more difficult to resolve. The supervisor is stymied and cannot decide. This cognitive dissonance (Festinger, 1957) is created by conflicting goals:

a. Approach-approach: the supervisor has two positive but mutually exclusive possible outcomes to a problem. For example, a faculty administrator (department chair) simultaneously being offered two similar deans' positions.
b. Approach-avoidance: the supervisor's decision contains both positive and negative outcomes. For example, the removal of a problem employee who was a long-term worker and good friend.
c. Avoidance-avoidance: the supervisor has two negative but mutually exclusive possible outcomes to a problem. For example, the supervisor having to choose between working weekends or working the evening shift.

Supervisors can disentangle goal conflict through understanding the work of Herbert Simon (1976), an economist, who has taken the concept of diminishing returns and applied it to decision-making. Simply stated, there comes a point in time in trying to solve a problem when the additional time and expense expended in trying to reach the best solution is not worth the effort; the costs outweigh the benefits derived by obtaining the utmost result. Since most supervisors are dealing with numerous problems on a daily basis, and do not have unlimited time and resources, Simon (1976) found that most supervisors employed the first viable solution that they came across – "satisficing" behavior.

The underlying thought in satisficing that deals with goal conflict is that supervisors need to adopt the view that there are no best decisions and that making a decision that is good enough is better than making no decision at all. To employ this method, supervisors need to develop time lines and time limits on their problem solving based upon the importance of the decision in question -- obviously a decision to terminate an employee should take far more time (especially given the need to check with one's manager) than more routine decisions such as scheduling vacations.

Last, once supervisors solve a problem, they should not second guess, ruminate, or revisit the decision unless to learn from the results of that decision to solve the next problem. Supervisors need to act in the present while thinking about the future while learning from their past. They should not live in the past to the detriment of the present and the ruination of the future.

How Does One Effectively Deal With One's Problem Managers?

It goes without saying that if there are problem employees, there certainly may be problem bosses. Brown (1983) has suggested that manager-supervisor interactions or level interfaces (the interaction between parties with different organizational ranks) are distinguished by task interdependencies, unequal formal power and a shared organizational context. Problem managers are much more difficult to deal with than problem employees since formal power lies within their jurisdiction. Try firing your boss and see what happens! Supervisors are administrators that are caught in the middle - they are simultaneously a superior and a subordinate and have to deal with the fact that these roles are interchangeable.

Many problems between supervisors and their managers are caused by the expectation gap, the differences between what subordinates want from their managers versus what they actually receive. In order to reduce this expectation gap, Gabarro and Kotter (1980) believe that supervisors should manage not only their employees but their bosses as well. First, managing one's boss requires an understanding of the mutual dependency of that relationship. Supervisors need to understand both themselves and their managers' strengths, weaknesses, motivation, and work habits in order to develop a working relationship based upon mutual trust and respect. Second, although it is natural for subordinates to be more dependent upon their superiors, it is probably a good idea that the subordinate be neither overly dependent nor overly independent.

According to Gabarro and Kotter, in poor relationships, the junior administrator can develop and manage the relationship through the development of compatible works styles, the aligning of mutual expectations, managing the boss's information flow, being trustworthy and dependable, and efficiently using the boss's time. In this case the responsibility for creating a better alignment between superior and subordinate must be on the subordinate (the academic supervisor), who must adapt his or her management style to fit the boss's style.

Brown (1983) slightly disagrees with Gabarro and Kotter in that he observed that a certain amount of tension or conflict between levels is normal and to be expected given power differences. Supervisors should anticipate and help manage this conflict through negotiation and facilitation while avoiding power struggles, dominance or submission behaviors, and abdication or apathy behaviors (too little conflict). These conflict resolution strategies can be translated into the TA nomenclature: power struggles is very similar to parent-parent behaviors, dominance or submission is very similar to parent-child behaviors, abdication or apathy is very similar to child-child behaviors, and negotiation and facilitation is characteristic of adult-adult behaviors. By referring back to TA, trying to institute an adult-adult relationship with one's boss, as well as one's own subordinates, is the most appropriate course of action.

Where Does the Supervisor go for Help with a Problem Manager?

Assuming that the supervisor has tried to first adapt to his or her manager's style and failing that, has tried to confront the manager with the problem, the sad truth is that there are but a few options left to the supervisor.

First, the supervisor should exercise patience. Just as supervisors may have their own style of managing and their own daily work routine, so too do their bosses. Second, consult with peer supervisors under the same manager to see how they deal with this manager. This tactic can produce a variety of results. First, these peers may not have the same problems with this manager or may have developed better coping and accommodation skills. Second, these colleagues can verify that they too are having problems and perhaps can develop a joint plan for confronting the manager in question. Third, the supervisor might need to be willing to move on to another position. Some working relationships are just not going to work out no matter how hard both parties try. Last, if the supervisor is not prepared to transfer to another position and can not tolerate the work situation, Davis and Lawrence (1977) tell us that the supervisor might consult with the manager's superior or, if appropriate, a union representative. Supervisors should realize that this is a most drastic measure, sometimes referred to as whistle-blowing, and may have tremendous negative repercussions for all parties involved, especially the supervisor.

So, Why Would Anyone Want to Supervise in a College or University?

Throughout this book, we have talked about the role of being a supervisor in a college or university environment. While we have identified many of the pitfalls that a supervisor in an academic or support role may face, we hope we have also identified many of the rewards and fulfilling opportunities that are also part of this exciting job. After all, we firmly believe that it is a privilege to be associated with a college or university, in either an academic or support capacity.

Being part of the academy can be extremely rewarding. The academy is one of the crucial pillars of our society, and being in a position to positively impact its activities is a rare opportunity that an academic or support supervisor will ever experience.

Helping to shape meaningful change can make it all worthwhile. Being in a position to make things better is part of this rare privilege. For certain, as we enter more deeply into the Information Age, things are different and changing all the time. Colleges and universities, as historic information organizations, are now facing new challenges as they seek to live in a more competitive environment and meet the needs of today's learners. Having the opportunity to positively impact what the programs of the future will be is extremely satisfying and rewarding. Both academic and support supervisors are on the leading edge of this revolution.

The Servant-Leader in Academics: Supervision is it Own Reward

Being able to help others be effective is an amazing reward in and of itself. Beyond planning and visioning what can be, a true reward of supervision is the opportunity to guide and nurture others. While it may be difficult to guide and direct professors (sometimes referred to as analogous of herding cats), academic supervisors still can mentor, guide, and influence. For other supervisors throughout the campus, the challenges are different, but fortunately, not unlike those of the traditional business world – so there are lots of successful examples to follow. Regardless, being able to work with and influence others and to see those efforts culminate in campus-wide (as well as individual) achievements is extremely fulfilling.

Helping the campus run better and more efficiently is effort nobly expended. As we have affirmed throughout, no campus has more resources than it needs. Further, it is unlikely that this situation will get any better. So, one of the major challenges to a college or university manager is how to provide high quality services with fewer and fewer resources. While this sounds like a losing proposition, it need not be. There are many emerging technologies and well as reengineered human resource approaches which benefit everyone at lower costs. By keeping abreast of the changes that impact supervision and management, supervisors and managers can become effective change agents that do good things for the campus and its community.

The self-reward of being a supervisor is the satisfaction of having done one's best and in having helped others do theirs. This is the unique opportunity of the supervisor. It allows the best of a person's skills, knowledge, and abilities to impact campus direction and quality. Having achieved success here goes well beyond the individual, but helps the college or university succeed as well. What greater satisfaction is there than this?

✇ Additional Resources ❦

Academic Supervision
- Pohland, Paul A. (1976). "Perspectives on Instructional Supervision: The Model Muddle." Paper presented at the Annual Meeting of the American Educational Research Association (San Francisco, California, April 19-23, 1976). The ERIC Database (1966-1981) AN: ED122355; CHN: EA008084.
- Sergiovanni, T. J. (1984). *Effective Department Leadership.* Boston: Allyn & Bacon.ERIC Clearinghouse on Education Management http://eric.uoregon.edu/.

Achieving Objectivity
- Internet Encyclopedia of Philosophy http://www.utm.edu/research/iep/o/objectiv.htm.

Customer Service
- Lewis, Ralph G. and Douglas H. Smith (1994). *Total Quality in Higher Education.* Delray Beach, Fl.: St. Lucie Press, p. 93.

Higher Education Journals
- AAUP. *Academe: Bulletin of the American Association of University Professors.*
- Association for Institutional Research [AIR]. *Research in Higher Education.*
- AAHE and Ohio State University. *The Journal of Higher Education.*
- ASHE. *The Review of Higher Education: The Journal of the Association for the Study of Higher Education.*
- National Education Association. *Thought and Action.*
- SCUP. *Planning for Higher Education.*
- *The Chronicle of Higher Education.* http://chronicle.com/.

Problem Solving and Creativity
- Amabile, T.M. (1983). *The Social Psychology of Creativity.* New York: Springer-Verlag. Creative Education Foundation. http://www.cef-cpsi.org/
- Tutorial on Brainstorming, Creativity and Innovation. http://www.infinn.com/ creative.html.
- Professional Associations and Unions American Association for Higher Education (AAHE) http://www.aahe.org/.
- American Association of University Professors (AAUP) http://www.aaup.org/.
- American Federation of Teachers (AFT) http://www.aft.org/higher_ed/resolutions.html

- The Council of Higher Education Management Associations (CHEMA) http://chema-www.colorado.edu/
- International Association of Universities/UNESCO: Information Centre on Higher Education. http://www.unesco.org/iau/centre_gen.html.
- Society for College and University Planning (SCUP). http://www.scup.org/index.htm

Supervisory Skills
- Robbins, Stephen P. and David A. De Cenzo (2001). *Supervision Today!* 3rd Edition. Upper Saddle River, N.J.: Prentice-Hall, Inc.
- Whetten, David A. and Kim S. Cameron (1993). *Developing Management Skills*. New York: HarperCollins College Publishers.
- Eight modules in developing key skills including: managing conflict, solving problems creatively, and managing stress. "Supervising and Supporting Your Staff." http://erc.msh.org/fpmh_ english/chp5/index.html.

Transactional Analysis
- The International Transactional Analysis Association's web page is http://www.itaa-net.org/.

Bibliography

Adams, J. S. "Inequity in Social Exchange." In L. Berkowitz (ed.) *Advances in Experimental Psychology*. New York: Academic Press, 1965.

Argyris, C. *Interpersonal Competence and Organizational Effectiveness*. Homewood, Ill.: Irwin, Dorsey Press, 1962.

Aronson, E. *The Social Animal*. 3rd Edition. San Francisco, Ca.: W.H. Freeman and Company, 1980.

Barnard, C. P. *The Functions of the Executive*. Cambridge, Mass.: Harvard University Press, 1938.

Bennis, W. *Why Leaders Can't Lead: The Unconscious Conspiracy Continues*. San Fransicsco, Ca.: Jossey-Bass Publishers, 1989.

Bittel, L. R. *Skills Development Portfolio for What Every Supervisor Should Know: The Basics of Supervisory Management*. 4th Edition. New York: McGraw-Hill Book Company, 1980.

Blake, R. R. and Mouton, J. S. *The Grid for Sales Excellence: New Insights Into a Proven System of Effective Sales* (2nd ed.). New York: McGraw-Hill Book Company, 1980.

Bowen, D. D. and Nath, R. "Transactional analysis in OD: Applications within the NTL model", *Academy of Management Review* (January), 1978, 79-89.

Brown, L. D. *Managing Conflict at Organizational Interfaces*. Reading, Mass.: Addison-Wesley Publishing Company, 1983.

Burack, E. H. and Smith, R. D. *Personnel Management*. New York: West Publishing Company, 1977.

Carroll, S. J. Jr. and Schneier, C. E. *Performance Appraisal and Review Systems: The Identification, Measurement, and Development of Performance in Organizations*. Glenview, Ill.: Scott, Foresman and Company, 1982.

Carvell, F. J. *Human Relations in Business* (3rd ed.). New York: Macmillan Publishing Co., Inc, 1980.

Certo, S. C. *Modern Mangement* (8th ed.). Upper Saddle River, N.J.:Prentice Hall, 2000.

Conger, J. A. and Kanungo, R. N. *Charismatic leadership in organizations*. Thousand Oaks, CA.: Sage Publications, 1998.

Coulter, M. *Strategic Management in Action* (2nd ed.). Upper Saddle River, N.J.: Prentice-Hall, 2002.

Davis, S. M. and Lawrence, P. R. *Matrix*. Reading, Mass.: Addison-Wesley Publishing Co, 1977.

Drucker, P. F. *People and Performance: The Best of Peter Drucker on Management.* New York: Harper's College Press, 1977.

Dunnette, M. D. *Personnel Selection and Placement.* Belmont, Ca.: Brooks/Cole Publishing Company, 1966.

Dyer, W. G. *Team Building: Issues and Alternatives.* Reading, Mass.: Addison-Wesley Publishing Company, 1977.

Elbing, A. O. *Behavioral Decisions In Organizations.* Glenview, Ill.: Scott, Foresman and Company, 1970.

Ellis, D. J. and Pekar, P. P., Jr. *Planning Basics for Managers.* New York: Amacom Books, 1980.

Etzioni, A. *Modern Organization.* Englewood Cliffs, N.J.: Prentice-Hall, Inc, 1964.

Festinger, L. *A Theory of Cognitive Dissonance.* Stanford, Ca.: Stanford University Press, 1957.

French, W. L. and Bell, C. H. *Organization Development: Behavioral Science Interventions for Organization Improvement* (5th ed.). Englewood Cliffs, N.J.: Prentice-Hall, Inc, 1995.

Fujishin, R. *Creating Effective Groups: The Art of Small Group Communication.* San Francisco, CA.: Acada Books, 2001.

Gabarro, J. J. and Kotter, J. P. "Managing Your Boss" *Harvard Business Review,* 1980, 58(1).

Galbraith, J. R. *Organizational Design.* Reading, Mass.: Addison-Wesley Publishing Co., 1977.

Gitlow, H., Oppenheim, A., and Oppenheim, R. *Quality Management: Tools and Methods for Improvement.* Burr Ridge, Ill: Irwin, 1995.

Goldman, E. "The Significance of Leadership Style." *Educational Leadership.* 1998, 55(7), 20-22.

Gouldner, A. W. *Patterns of Industrial Bureaucracy: A Case Study of Modern Factory Administration.* New York: The Free Press, 1954.

Griffin, R. W. *Task Design: An Integrative Approach.* Glenview, Ill.: Scott, Foresman and Company, 1982.

Hackman, J. R. and Oldham, G. R. *Work Redesign.* Reading, Mass.: Addison-Wesley Publishing Company, 1980.

Hage, J. and Powers, C. H. *Post-Industrial Lives: Roles and Relationships in the 21st Century.* Newbury Park, CA.: Sage Publications, 1992.

Halloran, J. and Benton, D. *Applied Human Relations: An Organizational Approach.* 3rd Edition. Englewood Cliffs, N.J.: Prentice-Hall, Inc., 1987.

Halloran, J. and Frunzi, G. L. *Supervision: The Art of Management.* (2nd ed.). Englewood Cliffs, N.J.: Prentice-Hall, Inc, 1986.

Harris, T. A. *I'm OK – You're OK: A Practical Guide to Transactional Analysis.* New York: Galahad Press. 1999.

Hersey, P. and Blanchard, K. R. *Management of Organizational Behavior: Utilizing Human Resources.* (6th ed.). Englewood Cliffs, N.J.: Prentice-Hall, Inc, 1993.

Housel, D. J. *Team Dynamics.* Cincinnati, Ohio: South-Western Publishing, 2002.

Howell, W. S. *The Empathetic Communicator.* Belmont, Ca.: Wadsworth Publishing Co., 1982.

Ivancevich, J. M. *Human Resource Management.* (8th ed). New York: McGraw-Hill Irwin, 2001.

Johnson, R. A., Kast, F. E., and Rosenzweig, J. E. *The Theory and Management of Systems.* New York: McGraw-Hill Book Company, 1963.

Katz, R. L. "Skills of an Effective Administrator", *Harvard Business Review* Sept/Oct, 1974.

Kaufmann, C. B. *Man Incorporate: The Individual and His Work in an Organized Society.* Garden City, N.Y.: Doubleday Anchor Books, 1969.

Kerr, S. "On the Folly of Rewarding A, While Hoping for B." *Academy of Management Journal*, 18(3), 1975, 769-83.

Kopelman, R. E. *Managing Productivity in Organizations: A Practical, People-Oriented Perspective.* New York: McGraw-Hill Book Company, 1986.

Kotter, J. P. *Organizational Dynamics: Diagnosis and Intervention.* Readings, Mass.: Addison-Wesley Publishing Company, 1978.

Lawrence, P. R. and Lorsch, J. W. *Developing Organizations: Diagnosis and Action.* Reading, Mass.: Addison-Wesley Publishing Company, 1969.

Lewin, K. *Field Theory in Social Science.* (D. Cartwright, Ed.) New York: Harper & Row, 1951.

Lewis, R. G. and Smith, D. H. *Total Quality in Higher Education.* Delray Beach, Fl.: St. Lucie Press, 1994.

Likert, R. *The Human Organization: Its Management and Value.* New York: McGraw-Hill Book Company, 1967.

Luft, J. "The Johari Window" *Human Relations Training News*, 5, 1961, 6-7.

Lussier, R. N. and Achua, C. F. *Leadership: Theory, Application, Skill Development.* Cincinnati, Ohio: South-Western College Publishing, 2001.

Luthans, F. *Organizational Behavior.* (8th ed). New York: McGraw-Hill Book Company, 1998.

Machiavelli, N. (trans. D. Donno). *The Prince and Selected Discourses: Machiavelli.* New York: Bantam Books, 1966.

McClelland, D. C. *The Achieving Society.* Princeton, N.J.: Van Nostrand, 1961.

McFarland, D. E. *The Managerial Imperative: The Age of Macromanagement.* Cambridge, Mass.: Ballinger Publishing Company, 1986.

McGil, M. E. *Organization Development for Operating Managers.* New York: Amacom, 1977.

McGregor, D. *The Human Side of Enterprise.* McGraw-Hill Book Company, Inc, 1960.

McKeachie, W. J. *Teaching Tips: A Guidebook for the Beginning College Teacher* (8th ed.). Lexington, Mass.: D.C. Heath and Company, 1986.

Mintzberg, H. *The Nature of Managerial Work.* Englewood Cliffs, N.J.: Prentice-Hall, Inc, 1973.

Mintzberg, H. *The Structuring of Organizations.* Englewood Cliffs, N.J.: Prentice-Hall, Inc, 1979.

Morrison, J. H. and O'Hearne, J. J. *Practical Transactional Analysis in Management.* Reading, Mass.: Addison-Wesley Publishing Company, 1977.

Odiorne, G. S. *How Managers Make Things Happen.* Englewood Cliffs, N.J.: Prentice-Hall, Inc, 1961.

Odiorne, G. S. *Management by Objectives: A System of Managerial Leadership.* New York: Pitman Publishing Corporation, 1965.

Osborn, A. F. *Applied Imagination: Principles and Procedures for Creative Thinking.* New York: Charles Scribner's Sons, 1953.

Ott, J. S. *The Organizational Culture Perspective.* Pacific Grove, Ca.: Brooks/Cole Publishing Company, 1989.

Ouchi, W. G. *Theory Z: How American Business Can Meet the Japanese Challenge.* New York: Avon Books, 1981.

Peter, L. J. and Hull, R. *The Peter Principle.* New York: William Morrow and Company, Inc, 1969.

Peters, T. J. and Waterman, R. H. Jr. *In Search of Excellence: Lessons from America's Best-Run Companies.* New York: Harper & Row, Publishers, 1982.

Peters, T. *The Circle of Innovation: You Can't Shrink Your Way to Greatness.* New York: Alfred A. Knopf, Inc, 1977.

Pfeffer, J. *Organizations and Organization Theory.* Boston, MA.: Pitman Books Ltd., 1982.

Pfeffer, J. and Salancik, G. R. *The External Control or Organizations: A Resource Dependence Perspective.* New York: Harper and Row, 1978.

Pfiffner, J. M. and Frank P. Sherwood, F. P. *Administrative Organization.* Englewood Cliffs, N.J.: Prentice-Hall, Inc., 1960.

Pinder, C. C. *Work Motivation: Theory, Issues, and Applications.* Glenview, Ill.: Scott, Foresman and Company. 1984.

Rawls, J. *A Theory of Justice.* Cambridge, Mass.: Harvard University Press, 1971.

Ronen, S. *Flexible Working Hours: An Innovation in the Quality of Work Life.* New York: McGraw-Hill Book Company, 1981.

Rothlisberger, F. J. & Dickson, W. J. *Industrial Worker.* Cambridge, MA: Harvard University Press, 1938.

Rowley, D. J. and Sherman, H. *From Strategy to Change: Implementing the Plan in Higher Education.* San Francisco, Ca.: Jossey-Bass, 2001.

Sargent, A.G. *The Androgynous Manager: Blending Male & Female Management Style's for Today's Organization.* New York: Amacom, 1983.

Scholtes, P. R. 1998. *The Leader's Handbook: A Guide to Inspiring Your People and Managing the Daily Workflow.* New York: McGraw-Hill, 1998.

Simon, H. A. *Administrative Behavior: A Study of Decision-Making Processes in Administrative Organization.* (3rd ed.). New York: The Free Press, 1976.

Spencer, L. J. *Winning Through Participation: Meeting the Challenge of Corporate Change With the Technology of Participation.* Dubuque, Iowa: Kendall/Hunt Publishing Company, 1989.

Steers, R. M., Porter, L. W., and Bigley, G. A. *Motivation and Leadership at Work.* (6th ed.). New York: The McGraw-Hill Companies, Inc, 1996.

Taylor, F. W. *The Principles of Scientific Management.* New York: Harper & Row, 1947.

Thompson, J. D. *Organizations in Action.* New York: McGraw-Hill Book Company, 1967.

Timm, P. R. *Supervision.* New York: West Publishing Company, 1984.

Timm, P. R. and Peterson, B. D. *People at Work: Human Relations in Organizations.* New York: West Publishing Company, 1982.

Timm, P. R. and Peterson, B. D. *People at Work: Human Relations in Organizations* (2nd ed.). New York: West Publishing Company, 1986.

Tubbs, S. L. *A Systems Approach to Small Group Interaction.* (2nd ed.). Reading, Mass.: Addison-Wesley Publishing Company, 1984.

Walsh, D. J. and Schwartz, J. L. "State Common Law Wrongful Discharge Doctrines: Update, Refinements, and Rationales" *American Business Law Journal* Summer, 1996, 645-689.

Waterman, R. H. Jr. *The Renewal Factor: How the Best Get and Keep the Competitive Edge.* Toronto, Canada: Bantam Books, 1987.

Weber, M. *Theory of Social and Economic Organizations* (in Henderson, A.M. & Parsons, T. ed.s and translators). London: Oxford University Press, 1947.

Weick, C. E. *The Social Psychology of Organizing.* (2nd ed.). Reading, Mass.: Addison-Wesley Publishing Company, 1979.

Wexley, K. N. and Latham, G. P. *Developing and Training Human Resources in Organizations.* Glenview, Ill.: Scott, Foresman and Company, 1981.

Whyte, W. H. Jr. *The Organization Man.* New York: Simon and Schuster, 1956.

Wick, C. W. and Leon, L. S. *The Learning Edge: How Smart Managers and Smart Companies Stay Ahead.* New York: McGraw-Hill, Inc., 1993.

Wren, D. A. *The Evolution of Management Thought.* (4th ed.). New York: John Wiley and Sons, Inc., 1994.

Yukl, G. *Leadership in Organizations.* 3rd Edition. Englewood Cliffs, N.J.: Prentice-Hall, Inc., 1994.

Zand, D. E. *Information, Organization and Power: Effective Management in the Knowledge Society.* New York: McGraw-Hill Book Company, 1981.

The Authors

Daniel James Rowley is a Professor of Management and Chair of the Management Department at the Monfort College of Business at the University of Northern Colorado. He is the lead author of three previous scholarly books on strategic planning and strategic management in colleges and universities; a workbook in the same series; a book on academic supervision; and a forthcoming textbook on business strategic management with Dr. Sherman. He is also the author of numerous articles and presentations on these subjects. He has presented papers and seminars and held workshops on academic strategic planning nationally and internationally. He has served as Editor and as Associate Editor of the *Journal of Behavioral and Applied Management,* and has published book reviews and article reviews in several different journals. He received his B.A. from the University of Colorado at Boulder; his MPA from the University of Denver; and his Ph.D. from the University of Colorado at Boulder as well. In 2004 he was named the Wells Fargo Professor as well as the University of Northern Colorado Scholar of the Year. He lives in Greeley, Colorado with his wife, Barbara, and daughter, Rebecca.

Herbert Sherman is a Professor of Management and Coordinator of the Business and Accounting Programs at Southampton College - Long Island University where he teaches courses at the undergraduate and graduate level in strategic management, research methods, and business ethics. His academic interests include case writing, strategic planning and implementation, academic planning, and change management. His most recent publications include co-authored work with Dr. Rowley in the areas of strategic management in higher education. He is the former Editor of *the Journal of Behavioral and Applied Management* and is the current Editor of *The Case Journal.* Dr. Sherman received his B.A. in Political Science from City College of New York, his M.S. in Management Science from Polytechnic University, and his Ph.D. in Strategic Management from the Union Institute and University. He lives with his wife Amy, and his daughter Melissa, while his son Seth is attending the University of Texas – Austin.

Index

Achua, 70
Adams, 71
Administrative Unit, 27, 28, 30, 31, 74
Adult Role, 80
Adult-Adult Relationships, 25, 26, 34, 35, 38, 39, 41, 68, 83
American Promotional System, 1
Argyris, 68
Aronson, 65, 70
Barnard, 5, 33, 47, 49
Bell, 68
Bennis, 70
Benton, 45, 51
Bigley, 33, 47, 57, 71, 75
Bittel, 7, 59
Blake, 43
Blanchard, 33, 71
Brown, 22, 61, 82, 83
Carroll, 9, 56, 73
Carvell, 45
Certo, 2
Chain of Command, 3
Child Role, 23, 67, 68, 79
Child-Child Relationships, 26
Conceptual Skills, 48
Conger, 5
Coulter, 67
David, 84
Dickson, 6
Donno, 60
Drucker, 44
Dunnette, 55
Dyer, 36, 68
Dysfunctional Relationships, 25
Elbing, 51, 62
Ellis, 48

Employee Accountability, 35
Employee Assistance Program (EAP), 78
Equifinality, 35
Etzioni, 68
Fayol, 6
Festinger, 81
First Line Management, 2, 39
French, 68
Front-Line Management, 3
Frunzi, 59
Fujishin, 19
Gabarro, 82, 83
Galbraith, 8, 31, 48, 51, 58, 74, 79, 80
Gantt, 6
Gilbreth, 6
Gitlow, 48
Goldman, 5
Gouldner, 10
Griffin, 56, 69
Hackman, 74
Hage, 50
Halloran, 45, 51, 59
Hawthorne Studies, 6
Hersey, 32, 71
High Time, 37
Housel, 79, 80
Howell, 43
HRM (Human Resource Management), 37, 38, 39, 41, 73
Human Relations, 43, 47, 52, 59
Human Resource(s), 1, 3, 4, 7, 16, 19, 21, 23, 36, 62, 66, 67
Ivancevich, 77, 78
Ivanevich, 69

Johnson, 10
Kanungo, 5
Kast, 10
Katz, 41, 58
Kaufman, 69
Kerr, 73
Kopelman, 69, 75
Kotter, 48, 82, 83
Latham, 19, 35
Lawrence, 73, 84
Leon, 64
Lewin, 52
Lewis, 63, 76
Likert, 60
Locke, 35
Lorsch, 73
Luft, 70
Lussier, 70
Luthans, 77
Machiavelli, 40, 60
Management, 1, 2, 3, 4, 6, 7, 8, 14, 15, 16, 17, 21, 22, 23, 30, 31, 32, 34, 35, 37, 38, 39, 40, 42, 44, 45, 49, 50, 54, 55, 60, 73, 74, 75, 76, 83, 85
Management by Walking Around (MBWA), 44
Management Structure, 3
McClelland, 47, 65
McFarland, 66, 71
McGregor, 7, 17, 38, 54, 60, 68
McKeachie, 45
Mintzberg, 44, 50, 53, 73
Monitoring, 55, 56, 58
Morrison, 78
Mouton, 43
Objectivity, 47
Odiorne, 19, 48
O'Hearne, 78
Oldham, 74

Oppenheim, 48
Organizational Relationships, 21
Organizational Resources, 2, 18
Organizing, 4, 8, 18, 20, 28, 38, 41, 48, 49, 50
Osborn, 51
Ott, 72
Ouchi, 45
Parent-Child Transaction, 34
Parent-Child-Adult Model (PCA), 22
Parochialism, 9, 65
Paternalism, 22
Peak Performer, 12
Pekar, Jr., 48
Peter Principle, 1
Peter, 32
Peters, 18, 38, 45, 46, 52
Peterson, 45, 68
Pfeffer, 12, 14
Pfiffner, 50
Pinder, 19, 75
Porter, 28, 30, 33, 47, 57, 71, 75
Powers, 50
Principal Investigator, 16
Problem Solving, 3, 45, 61, 62, 64, 67, 68, 81, 82
Rawls, 47, 72
Rehabilitation, 77, 78
Rewards Systems, 72
Role Enactment, 41
Role Sets, 24, 25
Ronen, 75
Rosenzweig, 10
Rothlisberger, 6
Rowley, 13, 72, 76
Salancik, 12
Sargent, 57
Satisficing, 82
Schneier, 9, 56, 73

Scholtes, 6
Schwartz, 81
Sherman, 13, 72, 76
Sherwood, 50
Simon, 51, 61, 81
Smith, 63, 76, 77
Smith, Adam, 40
Span of Control, 49
Spencer, 7
Steers, 33, 47, 57, 71, 75
Strategic Management, 67
Supervision, 1, 2, 3, 4, 14, 15, 16, 17, 18, 21, 27, 30, 31, 32, 33, 36, 37, 38, 39, 40, 41, 44, 52, 53, 54, 55, 56, 58, 59, 60, 63, 65, 84, 85
Supervisor(s), 1, 2, 3, 4, 5, 7, 8, 9, 10, 11, 12, 13, 14, 16, 17, 18, 19, 20, 21, 22, 23, 24, 26, 28, 29, 30, 32, 33, 34, 35, 37, 38, 39, 40, 41, 42, 43, 44, 45, 46, 47, 48, 49, 50, 51, 52, 53, 54, 55, 56, 57, 58, 59, 60, 61, 62, 63, 64, 65, 66, 67, 68, 70, 71, 72, 73, 74, 75, 76, 77, 78, 79, 80, 81, 82, 83, 84, 85
Supervisory Management, 3, 4, 11
Supervisory Philosophies, 17
Supervisory Relationships, 26
Taylor, 3, 6, 20, 33, 43, 52
Thompson, 30, 43, 76
Timm, 45, 68, 69, 77, 79
Transactional Analysis (TA), 21, 26, 79, 80, 83
Tubbs, 59
Walsh, 81
Waterman, 18, 32, 45, 46, 52
Weber, 6
Weick, 47
Wexley, 19

Whyte, 69
Wick, 64
Wren, 6, 75
Yukl, 71
Zand, 18